How to Make Love and Dinner the Same Time

200 Slow-Cooker Recipes to Heat Up the Bedroom Instead of the Kitchen

REBECCA FIELD JAGER

Adams Media, Avon, Massachusetts

Published by
Adams Media, an F+W Publications Company
57 Littlefield Street, Avon MA 02322. U.S.A.
www.adamsmedia.com

ISBN: 1-58062-918-0

Printed in the United States of America.

J   I   H   G   F   E   D   C   B

Library of Congress Cataloging-in-Publication Data
Jager, Rebecca Field.
How to make love and dinner at the same time / by Rebecca Field Jager.
p   cm.
Includes index.
ISBN 1-58062-918-0
1. Electric cookery, Slow I. Title.
TX827.J34 2003
641.5'884—dc21
2003001030

This book is available at quantity discounts for bulk purchases.
For information, call 1-800-872-5627.

Dedication

To my friends, thanks for making me strong.
To my enemies, thanks for making me stronger.
To my husband and children, thanks for making me happy.
To my parents, thanks for making me.
With love

Table of Contents

v

Forewordplay

$\mathcal{I}$magine this. Your man comes home from work and the kitchen's clean, dinner's done. Enticed by the delicious aroma wafting from the slow cooker, he lifts the lid and takes a peek. *Mmm,* Sun-Dried Tomato Chicken Gumbo, his favorite. He calls your name. You do not respond. Intrigued, he walks toward the bedroom, and finds the door slightly ajar. He pushes it open . . . what does he see?

1. **You, curled up in bed, snoring softly under the covers.** After a workday from hell, you crashed and burned knowing full-well dinner wouldn't.
2. **No one.** You're doing the mall thing; he can grab a quick bite and pick up the kids at his mother's.
3. **A good-bye note.** Having finally carried out your threat of walking out the door and never coming back, you prepared a nice meal in case you change your mind.
4. **You, sprawled on the bed, wearing nothing but an apron.** To you, the only thing more fun than making love is making love and dinner at the same time.

If you can see yourself in any of these scenarios, read on.

Acknowledgments

Without the help of many people this book would be just an idea. Thanks so much to:

My editor, and dragon slayer, Kate Epstein, for her guidance, enthusiasm, and support, and whose laughter made writing the book such fun; the learned ladies of the copyediting department, Khrysti Nazzaro and Laura MacLaughlin, for their meticulous work; Art Director, Paul Beatrice, for designing such an original, arresting cover; Colleen Cunningham, for her engaging design of the book; and Eulala Connor, whose telling cover illustration leaves so much to our imaginations.

My agent, Michelle Tessler, for believing in my work and working so hard to make others believe in it too.

My parents, Desmond and Toni Field; my sister, Nancy Sherrit; and my friends, Carole Strome, Marcie Crozier, and David Crozier, who did so much it would take *another* book to put it into words.

My friends, Laurie Stephenson, Christiane Dini, Greg Christie, Darrell Pantalone, Branka Vidovic, and Dr. Azra Ali, for their

ix

encouragement, and for being honest enough to tell me if recipes or CrockTalks were tasteless.

Everyone who bravely tested recipes, and everyone who generously contributed recipes: Janny Jager, Huguette Marchand, Dawn Powell, Adrian Vogt, Walt Trumble, Maria Babalos, Carrie Webb, Mary Churillo, Curt Hanson, and Habeeb Rhyman.

And above all, the loves of my life: my husband, Dan Jager, the most supportive, good-natured man on the planet; and my children, indeed my greatest creations, Samantha and Trevor Gary, who gave up lots of Mommy-time so I could do my thing.

A Peek Between the Covers

This book contains everything you need to know about slow cooking—not everything there is to know (that would kill a sequel)—but enough information to ensure stellar results.

Wait a minute, I hear you thinking, didn't slow cookers go the way of feminine napkin belts? Aren't they old granny contraptions used to make runny stew? Oh contraire, my friend! Slow cookers are like birth control pills: liberating devices that let you do what you want, when you want, with whom you want—without worrying about a bun in the oven.

Here's the thing. A slow cooker operates at such a low temperature you can safely leave it unattended. This means that rather than spending the day slaving over a hot stove or baby-sitting a turkey while it roasts, you can earn a living, go to the gym, or write a Pulitzer Prize–winning novel.

Of course, you can also blow your time racking up credit cards, drinking wine, and doing nasty things with that young guy from the city's Parks & Rec crew. The point is: it's up to you.

If you're a good cook, this book will help you uphold that tradition but without all the work. People will think, how does she do it? Serve great meals and have a life.

If you're a virgin cook—or a lousy one—this may be the culinary

1

exposé of your dreams. Easy recipes. No fancy foreign *f* words like *fricassee* and *flambé*. And a sure-fire way to get the kids thinking you're the best thing since sliced bread, and Hubby thinking about lickin' your spoon. As an added bonus, this book will help you keep up with the neighborhood superwife. You know, the woman who shows up at your potluck with the mother of all dishes. The ever-so-humble hostess who throws dinner parties billed as nothing fancy, but by 8 o'clock she's got the tenth course on the table and everybody's husband eating out of the palm of her hand. *Oh sure, you steam, I could cook like this too if I weren't so damn busy working, cleaning, shopping—doesn't anyone realize how long it takes to get half-decent highlights?* But, noooooo, you've got other obligations and interests, and besides, as a feminist, you're like, above cooking.

But even you gourmet chefs must admit it would be kind of cool to create delicious fare without being tied to the kitchen all day. To spend 15 minutes, say, throwing some stuff together in a pot, turning it on, and then taking off. When your family lines up at the trough, tah-dah, dinner is ready. And not mediocre mush, but truly delicious food.

With *How to Make Love and Dinner at the Same Time,* it's a breeze to cook for yourself, your family, your real—and so-called—friends. Hell, the Queen of Sheba could be coming for dinner and you'll be enjoying the afternoon at a spa. But when she parks her rear end at your table, not to worry. Your spread will be so appealing, it'll practically scream, *Eat me!*

The Advantages of Doing It Slowly

What do making love and making Rosemary Potato Pork Chops have in common? The slower the better. It seems that when juices have time to mix and flavors to blend, even the toughest turn out tender. Naturally, there's a lengthy scientific explanation about how, over time, low heat breaks down coarse particles, blah blah blah. But, suffice it to say, when a cold hard veggie lies down with an unyielding hunk of meat, and together they spend the afternoon side by side beneath a blanket of cream of potato soup, both become mellow, inseparable, one.

Don't believe me? Give it a try. I mean the recipe.

In addition to producing love-me-tender dinners, slow cooking offers many other benefits:

- **Beat the heat.** A slow cooker gives off little heat, so it won't turn your kitchen into an oven. It's ideal for scorching afternoons when you can't stomach the thought of another cold plate.
- **Cheap meat.** Low temperatures and long cooking times tenderize even the cheapest cuts of meat. Now you can put the savings toward real necessities, such as facials.
- **Low utility bills.** Slow cookers use very little energy. Now you can put the savings toward real necessities, such as more facials.
- **Less fat.** Unlike conventional cooking methods, slow cooking requires little oil or butter. Since great gobs of fat don't appear in the recipes, it stands to reason great gobs of fat won't appear on your thighs.

- **Crock-around-the-clock.** If you've got shift workers or party animals in your home, make them dinner before you go to bed. It'll be ready in the morning, and you'll be known as The Sleeping Saint.

- **99.9 percent burn-proof.** Slow cooking gives you a huge window of time to enjoy 1 postwork cocktail (or 2), with little risk of scorching supper.

- **Kidless dinners.** Because of the window-of-time thing, everyone in your family doesn't have to eat together. Feed the kids before afterschool activities and enjoy a peaceful dinner alone with hubby.

- **Prepare the night before.** If mornings are hell (*if?*), assemble dinner in the slow cooker the evening before, refrigerate it overnight, and then turn it on before leaving for work. To lessen your load, get your couch potato to peel his ancestors while he's watching prime-time TV.

- **Look beautiful while entertaining.** Since you're not stuck in the kitchen all day, you've got hours to get ready before guests arrive. Now you can soak in the tub, apply those expensive cosmetic samples you've been saving, shave where you've never shaved before, try on everything in the closet, shop for something new, and still have time to supervise your husband while he cleans the house.

- **Spend time banging other things than pots and pans.** Need I say more?

Finding Your Perfect Match

Slow cookers come in a variety of styles, so take your time select-ing. After all, you've got to wake up to it every morning and share personal space at night. Is it big enough for you? Do you enjoy pushing its buttons? How many mouths do you expect it to feed? And hey, even though it looks good now, will you want to take care of it when it's no longer shiny and new?

When choosing a slow cooker, it pays to shop around. Visit a store that displays appliances out of the box so you can inspect the equipment, minus fancy packaging. And remember, you must never succumb to that puppies-in-the-store-window feeling. You do not have to pick the first one that begs to be taken home.

Size Matters

This one's too small. This one's too big. Oh, this one's just right. Goldilocks obsessed over size and so should you. A slow cooker's dimensions determine how many people you can cook for, as well as the types of recipes you can try. Here's a rough guideline:

- 1 quart—ideal for dips and spreads and people who don't eat
- 2.5–3.5 quarts—geared for singles, DINKs, and empty nesters
- 3.5–5 quarts—feeds families of 3 to 5 people
- 5–7 quarts—great for larger families, as well as people big on entertaining or entertaining big people

Most slow cookers are round in shape, but some come in oval. Many cooks prefer an oval model because it fits an entire roast and you can do the funky chicken whole. Also, because a loaf tin or

6-cup round baking dish can be set into it easily, you can make custards and other difficult-to-remove dishes without suffering a meltdown.

What's Your Type?

A slow cooker is composed of a metal casing with heating coils that wrap around a stoneware insert. Your best bet is a removable insert, because it allows you to wash the insert separately without wrestling the entire appliance into the sink and risking electrocution. All models can be set at LOW (200°F) or HIGH (300°F). Fancy-dancy models also feature a WARM setting that the unit automatically switches to at the end of the cooking cycle. This is convenient if you're constantly running hours and hours behind, but it's certainly not a necessity. A regular slow cooker set on LOW will keep dinner waiting even if you're a few hours late.

Also worth mentioning are divided slow cookers. Either the stoneware itself is split in 2, or 2 inserts can be placed in the stoneware. If you have a thing against 1-pot meals, say, or beef mingling with carrots, this is an ideal model for you. It's also handy for creating 2 different side dishes or 2 different appetizers for a party. Best of all, a divided slow cooker lets you do half-and-half versions of the same meal. For example, a hearty stew for the meat-eaters—a meatless version for the vegetarians. Or, chili for the kiddies in one half—chili spiked with Magic Sex Potion in the half for Mom and Dad.

Looks Are Everything

Let's face it, the most important thing about any appliance is how it looks. Oh sure, quality's important, but everyone knows

1 ugly device can bring down an entire decor. First and foremost, your slow cooker must enhance the room.

For those who fancy themselves high-tech professional chefs, stainless steel models are available. Actually, stainless steel is good for people who fancy themselves period, as one can study one's reflection all day.

If you're after something more understated, a plain white model is nice. Clean and timeless, like you, it whispers: *I go with everything.*

If yours is a rustic kitchen, choose a slow cooker decorated with flowers or vines. Such shining samples of simplicity work well with fruit and veggie motifs or the duck/geese thing many country folk have happening.

When all is said and done, the most important thing to remember is this: Make sure you and your slow cooker can both turn each other on.

It's All in the Technique

What makes someone good at something? Is it years of experience or natural ability? A good chef is like a good lover: practice makes perfect, no matter what's in his genes.

To be a good slow-cooker chef you must get to know your appliance intimately. Its make, model, and size will cause it to respond differently. And while the recipes in this book provide a trustworthy guide, frequent use of your slow cooker will allow you to fine-tune cooking times perfectly. Perhaps your appliance is ready before most (premature). Maybe it needs a little longer (stamina). Find out by experimenting (*yee-ha!*).

Mastering a slow cooker is not the most challenging thing you'll do in your lifetime—one hopes—but there are a few things to remember:

Don't Flip Your Lid

The first time my mom used a slow cooker, she called me 100 times throughout the day.

"I don't think it's working," she fussed. "My potatoes are hard; my meat's undone."

"Leave it alone," I barked. "Every time you take the lid off to check it, you lose 20 minutes of cooking time."

Around 6 P.M., I ran out to pick up a pizza (did I say that?), so Mom was forced to leave a message on my machine. Due to heavy sobbing, the only word I could make out was "disaster."

I called home immediately. Dad answered.

"Dad, it's me."

"Who?"

"*Me.* Is everything okay?"

"Well, there's okay and then there's okay."

"Mom left a message. She seemed very upset."

"We haven't eaten. It's after 5."

"Geezus, Dad," I exploded. "I told her to leave that damn lid on the slow cooker! I specifically told her a million times!"

"Your mother can't let things be." Dad sighed. "Believe me, I know."

My parents ended up with grilled cheese sandwiches that night, but a fabulous beef stew was ready and waiting at 2 A.M.

Avoid Retaining Water

The only time it's necessary to remove the lid is to add ingredients near the end of the cooking cycle. When doing so, you'll notice considerable condensation trapped beneath. To avoid watering down your meal, carefully drain the condensation. A small bowl strategically placed next to the slow cooker works well for this purpose.

Meat on Top

Meat takes less time to cook than root vegetables such as potatoes, carrots, and turnips. To make sure everything is ready at the same time, place the veggies on the bottom, then pile the meat on top.

Give Breasts a Lift

When it comes to cooking poultry, white meat takes less time than dark. Gently place breasts on top of thighs and legs. (*Now breathe.*)

Avoid Frigidity

Always use fresh, or thoroughly thawed, meat or poultry. Not only is it unsafe to cook from frozen, it adds so much cooking time you'll be waiting for your roast beef until the cows come home.

Frequently Asked Questions

1. Do I look fat?
2. How much do you love me?
3. Who is better in bed: me or your last girlfriend?

Frequently Asked Questions about Slow Cooking

1. What's the difference between a slow cooker and a Crock-Pot®?

A Crock-Pot® is the brand name of the original slow cooker, invented by the Rival Company back in the '70s. The product was so successful it became a household name. For the purposes of this book, I cannot legally use it interchangeably. But, you go ahead.

2. Do I have to brown ingredients before adding them to the slow cooker?

To brown or not to brown, that is the question. Manufacturers say no, but chefs say yes. Why the disagreement? Prebrowning is time-consuming, so the folks who make slow cookers don't promote it. On the other hand, any gourmet chef will tell you browning enhances flavor and appearance. Me? I consider it a little like tidying up before the cleaning lady arrives, so it's not suggested in most of the recipes in this book. But, if time is not an issue, by all means, do it. In my mind, the time-savings/convenience benefits override the flavor/appearance ones, so I don't brown anything unless God is coming to dinner. And, She's bringing the pope.

3. Can I reheat leftovers in the slow cooker?

No, that's why humankind invented microwaves.

4. Can I cook pasta in a slow cooker?

Let's not go crazy. It's better to cook pasta in boiling water to not-quite-done tenderness, drain, and then add to your slow cooker. The exception is smaller pastas like stars and shells, which can be added uncooked to soups for the last 30 minutes or so, on HIGH.

5. What about rice?

Rice is fine in a slow cooker in most recipes, but make sure you use the long-grain converted kind.

6. **Can I use traditional recipes in my slow cooker?**

Sure, but there's a few things to keep in mind. Not as much liquid evaporates as it does when cooking on the stove or in the oven, so use 50 percent less liquid than your traditional recipe calls for. Dairy products don't hold up well, so they should be added toward the end of the cycle. Or, you can substitute a can of cream soup instead of, say, sour cream. Don't forget to increase the cooking time substantially—1 hour in the oven is approximately 6 to 8 hours in the slow cooker. Check it, though—I said *approximately.*

Slow Cookers Mean Never Having to Say You're Sorry

But . . . there are a few things to go over before you begin a recipe, just to make sure you and I are on the same page:

Ingredient size

Unless stated otherwise, use medium-sized fruits and vegetables. Slow cooking is not an exact science, but if you toss in a potato the size of Idaho, dinner *will* be starchy.

The peel deal

Peeling a potato is a matter of personal choice. Peeling an onion isn't. Unless stated otherwise, peel ingredients such as onions, carrots, parsnips, and garlic. Don't peel eggplants and zucchini as their edible skin helps keep their shape.

Combining ingredients

Ingredients do not have to be stirred while cooking. However, those of you prone to stir craziness will be happy to learn that often you must "combine" ingredients at the beginning of the recipe, which means stirring to mix them together.

Browning times and temperatures

Browning directions include specific times and temperatures such as "cook in oil over medium-high heat for 3 minutes." The type of skillet and stove you use affect the way things cook, so consider these directions accurate, but not rigid, guidelines.

Nonstick spray

For the most part, there is no need to grease your slow cooker before adding ingredients. However, supersticky dishes may call for a quick coating of nonstick cooking spray, which, to me, is the easiest greasing method. Those of you who must have a hand in everything may use margarine instead.

Cornstarch/flour

The water content of vegetables and the amount of fat in meat determine the volume of juices you'll end up with. Therefore, you may need to add more cornstarch or flour to a recipe to thicken it to your liking. Make sure you mix cornstarch with equal parts water prior to adding it to the slow cooker. When using flour, mix it with enough water to form a paste that is of pouring consistency, and stir it well until there are no lumps. To substitute cornstarch for flour or vice versa, keep in mind that 1 tablespoon of cornstarch equals 2 tablespoons of flour.

The salt factor

Salt is easier to add than take away, so recipes call for moderate amounts. Before you throw in extra, check the other ingredients. "Hidden" salt is found in canned goods such as broths, soups, sauces, and beans.

Chopping onions

Unless otherwise stated, use yellow cooking onions cut into little cubes about $1/8$- to $1/4$-inch in size. However you chop an onion is fine with me, but here's the fastest way:

1. Place a peeled onion on a cutting board, and cut in half from the root to stem.
2. Place 1 onion half cut-side down on the board and hold it steady by the root end.
3. Make parallel horizontal cuts toward the root, but do not cut through it.
4. Next, make vertical cuts from the stem to the root, again, not cutting through the root.
5. Finally, make cuts across the onion half, discard the root, and repeat with the other half.

Mincing garlic

Some people say no half-decent chef would be caught dead with a garlic press. I say go ahead and use one, but make sure you hide it. And, just in case anyone asks how you mince garlic, here's what to say:

1. I set an unpeeled clove on a cutting board, and press down on it with the blade of a knife. This loosens the peel so I can easily remove it.

2. Then, I crush the clove again.

3. To mince, I hold the handle of the knife in 1 hand and the tip of the knife on the board with the other, and move the blade across the garlic over and over again until it's almost a paste.

4. When I'm not mincing garlic, I'm churning butter, and plucking chickens I raise from scratch.

About the Recipes

In this book, not all recipes are created equal. Some are ideal for when you don't have time to think; most are geared for hectic-as-hell-but-nothing-unusual days; and others lend themselves to leisurely weekend mornings when you feel like cooking but don't want to get in too deep lest the moment passes. So that you know what you're getting into before you begin, look for one of the following symbols at the top of each recipe:

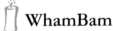

WhamBam   QuickEase   33 Minutes

WhamBam

In every section of this book, you'll notice a few WhamBam recipes. As the name implies, these are all about pulling out of the kitchen as quickly as possible. To qualify, a recipe must:

- Use 3 ingredients or fewer
- Have a preparation time of less than 7 minutes
- Require no prebrowning, broiling, or the use of any other appliance

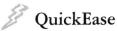 **QuickEase**

Most of the recipes are QuickEase, ideal for normally hectic days. To qualify, a recipe must:

- Use 4 or more ingredients
- Take less than 20 minutes to prepare
- Require the use of a slow cooker only

⏰ **33-Minute Recipes**

Here's some bad news: The average couple takes approximately 33 minutes to make love, including foreplay. The good news? That's the longest time it takes to prepare any recipe in this book. Oh, quit frowning, you're going to get wrinkles. The 33-Minute Recipes are not difficult; it's just that they require extra cooking steps such as browning, broiling, or puréeing. Examples include browning flour in a pan to make a roux to thicken gumbo, boiling pasta for a casserole, puréeing a soup, or popping a pie into the oven so its puff pastry topping can puff.

CrockTalks

When one of my friends drops by for a visit she almost always finds me in the kitchen, peeling, chopping, slicing, or dicing something. Usually, she grabs a cup of lukewarm coffee, plunks herself down at the kitchen table, and mumbles some offer to help. I go through the motions of protesting and she lies about liking to keep her hands busy while we talk. And, girl, do we talk. About men. About work. About men. About kids. About men. About clothes. About men. About memories. About men—well, you get the idea.

I'm not sure if it's the mindlessness of peeling, the rhythm of chopping, or the concentration required to measure spice, but there is something safe and comforting about preparing food, some sense of well-being evoked in the process that nurtures conversation, laughter, and, sometimes, tears. At the end of it all, the only thing ever fixed is dinner, but somehow problems seem lighter once they've been put on the table, sampled, and shared. Okay, *regurgitated*.

In any case, throughout this book, you'll find half-baked notions, random rants, and snippets of advice gleaned from the many years of kitchen conversations I've had with friends. I call these often-misguided entries CrockTalk because like chitchat, they warrant a simple name; they're not rocket science but mere morsels meant to amuse and entertain. Still, maybe you'll find a wee bit of inspiration among them. Sometimes it's just a little thing, like a pinch of cayenne pepper, that sets us on fire.

Teasers—Appetizers and Dips

There once was a time when you could go to a party and you weren't expected to bring a thing. Today's etiquette has it that not only do you have to bring your own booze, you must contribute an appetizer and sometimes even a hostess gift.

Kinda makes you not want to get invited out, huh?

All you can do is think of it this way: When it's your turn to entertain, you'll end up with a houseful of liquor, hors d'oeuvres, and vanilla-scented candles.

The trick to appetizers is knowing how to make a few of them really well. That way, when you're throwing a party you won't panic, or when you're called upon to bring one to a friend's, it won't ruin your day. On the contrary, you want to get it to the point where a frantic hostess calls requesting your specialty. *Sally,* she'll say. *Can ya bring your famous antipasto? My party will be a flop without it.* Or whatever.

The recipes in this section are not difficult, but the real beauty is your appetizer will be cooking while you're getting shampooed. And, trust me, as the hostess of many a party, these are the types of dishes that will always be welcome. On that note, allow me to suggest a few things you should NOT bring:

- Do not bring me store-bought frozen main courses. I have 1 oven, 2 racks, and 50 people to feed. A tray of frozen lasagna is not really an appetizer (even if I spend the evening cutting it into tiny servings), plus it will hog over an hour of precious oven time. What next? A frozen turkey?
- Do not bring me bags of chips, pretzels, cheese sticks, popcorn, peanuts, and all the rest of that crap. This is an adult

get-together. The magician and clown act were yesterday afternoon, next door. Of course, if you're male, you may ignore this pointer.

- Do not bring me a bag of groceries. A stick of pepperoni, a block of cheese, a bottle of olives, a package of mix, and a carton of sour cream do not a cheese-and-cracker plate make. I am the hostess. I am too busy to assemble your appetizer for you. And while I don't mind heating something in the microwave, the last thing I need is you in my kitchen asking where the plates, bowls, knives, whisk, and garbage are.

Caution: these pointers are only between you and me, and should not be written on your invitations.

Roasted Garlic and Black-Bean Dip

33 Minutes

An entire head of garlic, roasted to surprising sweetness, teams up with black beans, salsa, sour cream, and cream cheese to create a pretty pinkish dip ideal for tortilla chip dunking.

Yields 3 cups

1 head garlic, whole	½ cup sour cream
1 tablespoon olive oil	½ cup bottled salsa
1 (19-ounce) can black beans, rinsed and drained	¼ teaspoon ground cumin
	¼ teaspoon ground coriander
4 ounces cream cheese	¼ teaspoon cayenne

1. Preheat oven to 425°. Slice off the top ½-inch of the garlic head, exposing the tops of the cloves, and rub the entire head with the oil.
2. Place the garlic in an uncovered baking dish on the middle rack of the oven, and roast for 20 minutes.
3. Meanwhile, combine the remaining ingredients in the slow cooker.
4. Once cool enough to handle, squeeze the garlic pulp out of skins, and stir into the slow cooker.
5. Cook on LOW for 2 to 3 hours.
6. Transfer the mixture to a blender or food processor, and purée until smooth.
7. Return to the slow cooker, or serving dish, and serve warm.

 Tip: If an entire head of garlic sounds like too much, not to worry, garlic loses its strong flavor during the roasting process and becomes deliciously sweet!

Caramelized Red Onion Dip

QuickEase

A giant step up from conventional onion dip, this highly addictive version is heavenly with crackers, bread sticks, and Melba toasts.

Yields 3 cups
2 red onions, finely chopped
1$\frac{1}{2}$ teaspoons oil
1$\frac{1}{2}$ teaspoons brown sugar
1$\frac{1}{2}$ teaspoons red wine vinegar
8 ounces cream cheese
1$\frac{1}{2}$ cups sour cream
1 teaspoon lemon juice

1. Combine the red onions, oil, brown sugar, and red wine vinegar in the slow cooker.
2. Cook on LOW for 3 to 4 hours.
3. Stir in the cream cheese, sour cream, and lemon juice, and cook for an additional 1 to 1$\frac{1}{2}$ hours.
4. Chill, and bring to room temperature before serving.

 Tip: If possible, make this dip the day before you intend to serve it to allow time for the flavors to develop and blend. Calorie watchers may use light cream cheese and/or light sour cream in this recipe.

Addicted to Love

Ever notice when women get into relationships, we take on our lover's addictions? I'm not referring to a guy's vices, but rather, his hobbies and passions. Show me the contents of your storage closet and I'll show you a history of your boyfriends. Remember the guy who always wore cowboy boots? That's why you have country and western CDs. And the time you fell head over heels for that outdoor type? Look! There's your rock-climbing gear. And here's a magazine called *Choo-Choo Monthly.* Remember the guy who built model trains? And . . . *is that a studded, leather bra?* Remember the—oh, never mind. And look at all these relationship self-help books telling you how you can change! Seems like ultimately you decided not to—so let's take this junk out to the curb.

Easy Wine-and-Cheese Fondue

WhamBam

There's something about piercing a bit of bread or apple,
and dipping it into a warm sauce that will make you
and someone special want to feed it to each other.
Great for guests, but more fun for 2.

Serves 4
1 clove garlic, halved
1 1/2 cups dry white wine
1 pound Swiss Emmental cheese, grated

1. Rub the inside of the slow cooker with the garlic, and discard.
2. Pour the wine into the slow cooker, and cook on HIGH for 1 hour.
3. Add the cheese in batches, stirring constantly.
4. Cook for an additional 30 minutes on LOW.

 Tip: If the sauce requires thickening or begins to curdle, sprinkle in 1 or 2 tablespoons of flour, stir, and continue to cook. If you're wondering what Emmental cheese is, it's the stuff most people think of when they think of Swiss cheese—the pale yellow kind with the holes. Its mild, nutty flavor makes it a popular choice for fondues.

Warm Bean Salsa

QuickEase

A hot dip with plenty of kick, sure to spur on the party.
If you want to get the cowboys really rowdy,
add 1 or 2 pinches of cayenne.

Yields 4 cups
1 (19-ounce) can red kidney beans, rinsed and drained
1½ cups bottled hot chunky salsa
1 green onion, chopped
1 onion, diced
1 chili pepper, diced
1 clove garlic, minced
10 pimento-stuffed green olives, chopped
¼ teaspoon ground coriander
½ cup shredded Cheddar cheese

1. Combine all the ingredients *except* the cheese in the slow cooker.
2. Cook on LOW for 3 to 4 hours.
3. Using a potato masher, mash slightly, and sprinkle with cheese before serving.

 Tip: Chili peppers contain oils that can burn, so when preparing, wear plastic or rubber gloves to protect your skin and be very careful not to rub your eyes!

Fiery Artichoke-Zucchini Spread

QuickEase

Spicy cayenne takes a dip in a refreshing artichoke-zucchini blend.
Serve piping hot with thick slices of warm crusty bread.

Yields 4 cups

1 (14-ounce) can artichoke hearts, drained and finely chopped
1 small zucchini, grated
8 ounces cream cheese
1 cup sour cream
$1/4$ cup grated Parmesan cheese
1 green onion, finely chopped
1 teaspoon lemon juice
$1/4$ teaspoon cayenne

1. Combine all the ingredients in the slow cooker.
2. Cook on **LOW** for 2 to 3 hours, and serve hot.

 Tip: To grate zucchini, simply rub it against the large holes of a cheese grater.

How to Pick Up a Man in the Supermarket

Okay, ladies, we begin our lesson in the produce department. See the hoses spraying water on the salad stuff? Quickly stick your head under so you get that misty look. Now, saunter over to the melons and lift 2. Hold 1 in each hand, and cup them gently against your chest. Now, squeeze. Wonderful . . . let's move on to zucchini. Nothing vulgar here, ladies, you're trying to pick up a man, not a maniac. Simply grab a zucchini and hold it firmly enough so that you don't appear afraid, but with a touch of uncertainty so it doesn't look like you've handled millions. Very good. Okay, let's move on to meat. Wait! Don't hunch over your shopping cart as you push it—you're a hot chick, not a bag lady! Shoulders back, chest out, tummy in—lovely, let's proceed to tongues.

Honey-Garlic Cocktail Ribs

33 Minutes

Sweet and garlicky fall-off-the-bone ribs in a dark and sticky sauce. Beautiful on the buffet table . . . while they last.

Yields about 30
3 pounds pork spareribs, cut into single sections
3 cloves garlic, minced
3/4 cup honey
3 tablespoons soy sauce
1 teaspoon prepared mustard
1/2 teaspoon ground ginger
1/4 teaspoon hot pepper sauce

1. Broil the ribs for 20 minutes, turning them once.
2. Drain, and transfer the ribs to the slow cooker.
3. In a small bowl, combine the remaining ingredients, and pour over the ribs.
4. Cook on LOW for 4 to 6 hours, or on HIGH for 2 to 3 hours.

 Tip: These ribs can also be served as a main course for 4, along with fried rice and vegetables. Cut into 5-rib sections instead of single sections.

Sticky Wings

33 Minutes

Don't be surprised if these sweet, sticky, soy sauce–basted chicken wings fly off the table. Fabulous hot or cold.

Yields about 18
2 pounds chicken wings, split in half, tips removed
2 cups brown sugar
1 cup soy sauce
2 tablespoons hoisin sauce
$1/2$ teaspoon ground ginger
$1/4$ teaspoon garlic powder

1. Broil wings for 15 minutes, turning them once.
2. Meanwhile, in a saucepan, combine the remaining ingredients, and bring to a boil.
3. Reduce heat to medium-low, and let cook for 5 minutes.
4. Drain wings and transfer to the slow cooker; pour the soy-sauce mixture over the top, stirring to make sure all are coated.
5. Insert toothpick under the lid to pry it open slightly.
6. Cook on HIGH for 3 to 4 hours.

 Tip: If you want to save time, buy precut wings. If you want to save money, purchase whole wings; but rather than discard the tips, freeze them and use them in your next chicken broth.

Late-Night Curried Soy Nuts

QuickEase

The next time houseguests get a hankering for something crunchy while watching late-night TV, serve up a batch of these protein-loaded treats.

Yields 4 cups

4 cups roasted soy nuts
3 tablespoons butter, melted
1 tablespoon brown sugar
2 teaspoons curry powder
1/4 teaspoon ground cumin
1/4 teaspoon salt

1. Place the soy nuts in the slow cooker.
2. In a bowl, mix together the remaining ingredients.
3. Pour over the soy nuts, and stir until the nuts are coated well.
4. Cook on LOW for 2 hours.
5. Remove lid, and cook for an additional 30 minutes on LOW.

 Tip: Roasted soy nuts taste somewhat like peanuts and are available in bulk-food stores, health food stores, and larger supermarkets. If not available, use regular peanuts instead.

My To-Do List for Entertaining Overnight Guests

In addition to cleaning the entire house from top to bottom, including windows, walls, and hair in drains, I must:

1. Dump junk drawer and crap on top of fridge in box, and stick in basement.
2. Bribe kids to be nice to their kid even though he's a chess protégé.
3. Tell Hubby to fix towel-holder rod so it won't fall off.
4. Get mildew stains off bathroom ceiling. If can't, paint over.
5. Get stuff for breakfast: bacon, eggs, pancake mix, real maple syrup, strawberries, croissants, freshly squeezed orange juice, coffee beans (borrow grinder thingy), real cream, sugar cubes.
6. Buy matching cream-and-sugar set.
7. Buy night-table lamp.
8. Buy night table.
9. Look for pillowcase that goes with blue-flowered sheet set. If can't find, buy whole new set.
10. Ask Hubby if he can make spare room bigger.

Pizza Roll

Pepperoni, mozzarella cheese, and tomato sauce wrapped in deli-bought pizza dough. As it bakes, your kitchen fills with a lovely pizza-parlor aroma.

Serves 4
Flour
16 ounces prepared pizza dough
$^1/_2$ cup pizza sauce
1 cup shredded mozzarella cheese
1 cup thinly sliced pepperoni

1. Sprinkle work surface with flour.
2. With a floured rolling pin, roll the pizza dough into 9" × 12" rectangle.
3. Spread the pizza sauce on the dough, sprinkle with the cheese, and top with the pepperoni.
4. Beginning at the long end, roll up the dough into a log, and pinch the ends and seam together with a few drops of water to seal; make a slit on top for steam to escape.
5. Spray the slow cooker with nonstick spray, and carefully transfer roll to the slow cooker, wrapping ends together to fit.
6. Cook on HIGH for $2^1/_2$ to $3^1/_2$ hours or until slightly golden.
7. Remove from slow cooker, and let sit for 5 minutes before slicing.

 Tip: Prepared dough can be purchased in bags at the deli of many supermarkets.

Channna

A fabulous festival of texture and taste, as well as a healthful, light snack. Here, mashed chickpeas lend their nutty flavor to sweet bell peppers, onion, and spices.

Yields 4 cups

2 (19-ounce) cans chickpeas, rinsed and drained
2 green onions, diced
1 green pepper, diced
1 red pepper, diced
1 tablespoon brown sugar
1 teaspoon ground cumin
1 teaspoon curry powder
$1/2$ teaspoon cayenne pepper
$1/2$ teaspoon salt

1. Place the chickpeas in the slow cooker.
2. Mash with potato masher, leaving a few whole.
3. Stir in the remaining ingredients.
4. Cook on LOW for 3 to 4 hours.

 Tip: Serve with mini pita pockets, pitas cut into triangles, or crackers.

Antipasto Palette

33 Minutes

Even the most famous Italian artists would love this gorgeous palette of color and taste. Serve alone with crackers, or with olives, veggies, and cold meats.

Makes 4 cups
1 small eggplant, diced
1 plum tomato, peeled and diced
1 celery rib, finely chopped
1 carrot, finely chopped
8 green beans, finely chopped
10 pimento-stuffed green olives, finely chopped
10 pitted black olives, finely chopped
1/4 cup tomato sauce
4 tablespoons red wine vinegar
2 tablespoons olive oil
1 1/2 tablespoons brown sugar

1. To remove bitter juices, sprinkle the diced eggplant with salt; let drain in colander for 20 minutes, rinse, and pat dry.
2. Combine all the ingredients in the slow cooker.
3. Cook on LOW for 3 to 4 hours.
4. Chill, and serve.

 Tip: To peel a tomato, make a crisscross cut on the nonstem end, soak in boiling water for about 15 seconds, and pull the skin off.

Under My Skin

Sometimes, bitterness exists just beneath an eggplant's skin. That's why, before using one in a recipe, you should always cut or chop it according to the recipe's directions, sprinkle it with salt, and let it drain in a colander for 20 minutes or so. This process draws out the bitter juices so that after a thorough rinsing your eggplant is ready to roll! Hmm. Kind of reminds me of women. Let's face it, just below the surface of our lovely skin occasionally bitterness resides. And yet, if we plunge our bodies into a sea-salt bath and relax for a while, all that nastiness drifts away. A quick shower to rinse off the residue, and we too emerge refreshed, invigorated, clean. Seems like a good excuse for a day at the spa. Or at least a nice long soak before bed.

Sweet-and-Sour Meatballs

WhamBam

*Serve unexpected guests this tasty appetizer that consists of
only 3 ingredients: 1 bottled, 1 frozen, and 1 fresh.*

Yields 2 dozen

1 (24$\frac{1}{2}$-ounce) jar sweet-and-sour cooking sauce with
    pineapple
24 frozen, fully cooked meatballs
2 green peppers, chopped

1. Pour the sweet-and-sour sauce into the slow cooker.
2. Cook on HIGH for 45 minutes.
3. Add the meatballs and green peppers to the slow cooker
4. Cook for an additional 1 hour on HIGH.

Tip: Gone are the days when most of us have time to
prepare a bunch of appetizers from scratch, so don't feel
guilty taking advantage of the many "convenience"
foods available. If you'd like to add a homemade touch
to this recipe as well as some color, throw in a handful
of slivered carrots and red peppers with the meatballs.

Sourdough Toasts with Mushrooms

QuickEase

*Thick slices of toasted sourdough bread slathered with
a rich and creamy mushroom sauce. Makes an
awesome appetizer, or bedtime snack.*

Yields 8
4 cups chopped mushrooms
1 tablespoon Madeira
2 teaspoons lemon juice
1 teaspoon Dijon mustard
1 teaspoon mustard seeds
$1/4$ teaspoon pepper
$1/4$ teaspoon salt
2 tablespoons water *or* vegetable stock
3 tablespoons sour cream
4 slices sourdough bread, toasted

1. Combine all the ingredients *except* the sour cream and sourdough
   bread in the slow cooker.
2. Cook on LOW for 5 to 7 hours, or on HIGH for $2^{1}/2$ to $3^{1}/2$ hours.
3. Stir in the sour cream.
4. Spread the mixture onto slices of toast, cut into halves, and serve.

 Tip: If you purchase sourdough bread in a baguette form, slice
and toast, and serve mushroom sauce in a bowl surrounded by
toasts.

Portobello-Stuffed Canapés with Stilton

33 Minutes

Elegant pop-in-your-mouth canapés stuffed with roasted inky black portobello mushrooms buried beneath crumbles of blue cheese.

Yields 20

6 portobello mushrooms, finely chopped
1 clove garlic, minced
2 tablespoons finely grated onion
1 tablespoon olive oil
1/2 teaspoon pepper
2 tablespoons balsamic vinegar
Approximately 20 pieces prepared canapés
1/4 teaspoon salt
3 ounces Stilton cheese, crumbled

1. Combine the mushrooms, garlic, onion, olive oil, and pepper in the slow cooker.
2. Cook on LOW for 2 hours.
3. Stir in the balsamic vinegar and salt, and cook for an additional 15 minutes.
4. Meanwhile, arrange the canapés on a baking sheet. Fill each canapé with the mushroom mixture, and top with Stilton.
5. Broil for 2 or 3 minutes, until the cheese melts.

 Tip: Packages of prepared canapés are available in most supermarkets.

Where There's Smoke . . .

You're just about to kick off your dinner party with Portobello-Stuffed Canapés, and the broiler sets them on fire. Sniffing disaster, your female guests rush into the kitchen, slamming on their brakes like rubberneckers taking in an accident scene. How do you handle the situation? With style. Throw your head back and laugh gaily—ha! ha! ha!—and then utter some seemingly throwaway line like, *Oh heavens, I haven't burned anything since the first time I attempted Coquille St. Jacques!* Like those billows of smoke that hang in the air, this sentence will cloud the issue of your ability to make canapés with the more wondrous notion you know how to make even fancier cuisine. *Not to worry,* you then add with a smile. *You all go back to emptying my liquor cabinet and I'll have dinner ready in a jiffy.* Now focus (and this time, *really* focus) on the soup.

Chicken Bites in Thai Peanut Sauce

QuickEase

Let guests help themselves right from the slow cooker
to tender morsels of chicken breast drenched
in a coconut milk–peanut sauce.

Serves 6

1½ pounds chicken breast, boneless, skinless, cut into
    bite-size pieces
2 green onions, sliced
1 chili pepper, chopped
¼ cup crunchy peanut butter
2 tablespoons brown sugar
1 tablespoon soy sauce
½ cup chicken broth
½ cup coconut milk

1. Combine all the ingredients *except* the coconut milk in
   the slow cooker.
2. Cook on **LOW** for 3 to 4 hours.
3. Stir in the coconut milk, and cook for an additional
   30 minutes on **LOW**.

 Tip: If the sauce gets too thick, thin it with additional
coconut milk.

Brie with Red Pepper Jelly in Grape Leaves

33 Minutes

Warm bundles of grape leaves stuffed with Brie and red pepper jelly, and drizzled with lemon and oil. Not to worry, they just look complicated.

Yields 12

12 grape leaves

¼ pound Brie, cut into 12 cubes

¼ cup red pepper jelly

1 teaspoon olive oil

1 teaspoon lemon juice

1. Boil the grape leaves for 5 minutes; then drain, rinse, and pat dry.
2. Cut off the stems.
3. Lay the grape leaves flat on a work surface, shiny-side down.
4. Place a piece of Brie in the center of each leaf, and spread a bit of red pepper jelly over the Brie.
5. Wrap the Brie in the leaves: fold over base, tuck in the sides, roll up, and secure with toothpick.
6. Set the bundles in a 6-cup baking dish in a single layer, and place the dish in the slow cooker.
7. Drizzle olive oil and lemon juice over the bundles.
8. Cook for 1 to 1½ hours on LOW.

Tip: Look for jarred grape leaves in supermarkets and specialty food stores.

The Last of the Wrap Stars

Would somebody tell me why gift bags are so popular? Sure, they're convenient for the giver, but they're such a rip-off to receive. Let's face it, how much fun can I have opening a bag? There's no bows or wrapping paper to tear off, no bits of tape to prolong the joy. And half the time, those tufts of tissue paper don't properly hide the gift so that when the bag gapes open, it ruins the surprise. And those itty-bitty cards attached to their handles? How can you possibly express how much I mean to you on such a limited space? Worst of all, you didn't even pay for the gift bag. Somebody gave it to you, and you decided a wrinkly old bag was good enough for me! Excuse me? I gave it to you on your last birthday? Oh.

Prune Pockets Stuffed with Wild Rice and Smoked Turkey

QuickEase

Beneath a sprinkling of fresh chives, warm wild rice and tender bits of smoked turkey breast snuggle up in cozy little pockets of prunes.

Yields 24

$^1\!/_2$ cup wild rice, uncooked

2 ounces smoked turkey breast, diced

$^1\!/_4$ teaspoon nutmeg

$^1\!/_4$ teaspoon pepper

$^1\!/_4$ teaspoon salt

1 cup chicken broth

24 jumbo or extra-jumbo prunes, pitted

2 tablespoons chopped fresh chives

1. Combine all the ingredients *except* the prunes and chives in the slow cooker.
2. Cook on LOW for 6 to 8 hours.
3. Slice open the prunes lengthwise to create "pockets," being careful not to slice completely through.
4. Stuff the rice and turkey mixture into the prune pockets, sprinkle with chives, and serve.

 Tip: This dish is also delicious served cold, so if you prefer, prepare it in advance, and chill until ready to serve.

Sip into Something Comforting—Soups

recipe list continued on following page

37

*A*h, soup. Just the thought of it makes you want to crack open a can. Well, listen my little condensed connoisseur, by the time I get done with you, your name shall be SouperWoman, bearer of all things good.

Girl, if there's one thing you need to do in this lifetime, it's learn how to make a half-decent pot of soup. Why? Because it's a pathetically easy way of showing off your culinary skills, whether they're plentiful, or few. With soup, there are no rules. It can be thick or runny, brimming with ingredients or as sparse as a cup of tea (some clever chef named this consommé). It can be made with a few bones, wilted veggies, and water, or the greatest riches of the land and sea. It can be served for lunch or dinner, as a first or main course. And it can be ladled piping hot from the slow cooker, microwaved the next day, or frozen, then reheated for a future last-minute supper.

Best of all, soup captures your mood. It shows the world who you wish to be that day. Nothing whispers *Come to Mama* like a mug of Healing Chicken Soup; nothing proclaims *My God I'm hip* like a bowl of Mellow Yellow Corn Soup with Saffron. And if you're looking to get lucky, just uttering the word *bouillabaisse* forces your lips into such an appealing pucker, one can only imagine what will happen to you when you break out the Tropical Pepper Pot.

We begin this section with broth. Yes, cartons, cans, and cubes are acceptable for all the soups in this section, but when the broth is the star attraction, such as in Pearl Soup or French Onion, promise me you'll attempt a broth from scratch. In fact, from now on, promise me you'll make all your soups homemade. That you will throw into your cauldron an orgy of ingredients, and let them brew for hours until each has expended every last drop of its being into what will no doubt be a culinary masterpiece. Oh all right, promise me you'll do it sometimes.

And promise me, once you are known as SouperWoman, your head won't swell as your husband smothers you with compliments and your girlfriends gag with envy. No, promise me you will maintain your modesty and simply explain that while there's nothing wrong with canned soups per se, personally, you prefer to serve your family homemade.

People will hate you. It's gonna be great.

Dark and Delicious Beef Broth

QuickEase

Choose bones with a bit of meat for full-out flavor. Excellent in soups, stews, casseroles, and over pot roast.

Yields 8 cups
4 beef bones
2 onions, roughly chopped
2 carrots, unpeeled, roughly chopped
2 celery stalks with leaves, roughly chopped
5 whole peppercorns
3 teaspoons dried parsley
$1/2$ teaspoon salt
1 bay leaf
8 cups water

1. Combine all the ingredients in the slow cooker.
2. Cook on LOW for 12 to 14 hours.
3. Strain through a colander lined with cheesecloth.
4. Discard the bones and vegetables.
5. Once cool, skim off fat.

 Tip: Cheesecloth is thin, loosely woven cloth sold in the kitchen accessories section of supermarkets and department stores.

Homemade Chicken Broth

QuickEase

Hours of slow cooking pay off in a deep golden broth ready to add homemade authenticity to a bizillion culinary pleasures.

Yields 8 cups
3 pounds chicken parts (necks, backs, thighs, legs)
2 carrots, unpeeled, roughly chopped
2 celery stalks with leaves, roughly chopped
1 onion, halved
1 teaspoon dried basil
1/2 teaspoon dried oregano
6 peppercorns, whole
1/4 teaspoon salt
1 bay leaf
8 cups water

1. Combine all the ingredients in the slow cooker.
2. Cook on LOW for 12 to 14 hours.
3. Strain through a colander lined with cheesecloth.
4. Debone the chicken and reserve for other use; discard bones and vegetables.
5. Once cool, skim off fat.

 Tip: Use the chicken meat in Healing Chicken Soup, or other recipes calling for cooked chicken.

Nature's Veggie Broth

QuickEase

A garden of ingredients makes up this vegetarian's dream that is rich in flavor and color.

Yields 8 cups

3 carrots, unpeeled, roughly chopped

3 celery stalks with leaves, roughly chopped

2 cloves garlic, unpeeled, crushed

1 leek, chopped

1 parsnip, unpeeled, roughly chopped

1 onion, quartered

6 whole peppercorns

1 teaspoon salt

1/2 teaspoon dried thyme

1/2 teaspoon dried parsley

1 bay leaf

8 cups water

1. Combine all the ingredients in the slow cooker.
2. Cook on LOW for 12 to 16 hours.
3. Strain through a colander lined with cheesecloth, pressing vegetables gently.
4. Discard vegetables.

Tip: Different types of vegetables can be used, such as shallots, turnips, or cabbage. Avoid stronger tasting vegetables such as Brussels sprouts and broccoli. Potatoes add flavor, but they do create a more cloudy broth.

Pearl Soup

QuickEase

Pearl onions, pearl barley, and an ensemble of white ingredients shimmer like stars in the dark winter sky. Serve with a fresh snowfall of Parmesan.

Serves 8

3 potatoes, diced

3 pearl onions, quartered

2 parsnips, sliced

1 (19-ounce) can navy *or* white
kidney beans, rinsed and drained

3/4 cup pearl barley

1/4 teaspoon white pepper

8 cups beef broth

Freshly grated Parmesan cheese

1. Combine all the ingredients *except* the Parmesan in the slow cooker.
2. Cook on LOW for 6 to 8 hours, or on HIGH for 3 to 4 hours.
3. Serve with Parmesan cheese.

 Tip: Grating Parmesan into your soup sort of makes you feel like you're dining out, so purchase it in blocks, if available.

Buyer Beware . . .

Even women dripping pearls can be cheapskates who constantly stick others with the restaurant tab. Here's how they do it:

1. Just before the check arrives, the cheapskate politely excuses herself to the washroom.
2. When she returns, she avoids eye contact with the check, even if it's in clear view on the table.
3. No matter how long she and her companion chitchat, she will not break down and acknowledge that nasty little piece of paper. She's waiting for her companion to pick it up—possession being nine-tenths of the law.
4. Once her companion has the check in hand, the cheapskate offers to get it. But suddenly, she loses control of her fine motor skills! She fumbles with her purse clasp, can't find the right credit card . . . in the meantime, her companion pays.
5. She promises to treat next time.
6. Back to number 1.

French Onion Soup

33 Minutes

With a little help from the broiler, you can serve this popular soup of caramelized onions and beef broth beneath a blanket of toasted bread and melted cheese.

Serves 8

2 pounds onions, thinly sliced
$^{1}/_{4}$ cup butter, melted
1 tablespoon sugar
6 cups beef broth
$^{1}/_{2}$ cup dry white wine (optional)
$^{1}/_{2}$ teaspoon pepper

$^{1}/_{4}$ teaspoon salt
1 small baguette, cut into $^{1}/_{2}$-inch slices
1$^{1}/_{2}$ cups shredded mozzarella *or* Gruyère cheese
$^{1}/_{2}$ cup grated Parmesan cheese

1. Combine the onions, butter, and sugar in the slow cooker.
2. Cook on LOW for 4 hours.
3. Add the broth, wine, pepper, and salt, and cook for an additional 3 to 4 hours.
4. Ladle the soup into ovenproof bowls, place 2 baguette slices on each, and sprinkle with cheeses.
5. Broil for a few minutes until the cheese melts.

 Tip: Caramelizing the onions enhances the flavor, but if you're going to be out all day, throw everything in at the beginning, and broil with bread and cheeses when you get home.

ABC Hamburger Soup

33 Minutes

Cast a spell with letter pasta in a mild tomato broth laced with crumbled beef. Your little ones will love it . . . and so will the big guy.

Serves 6
1 pound lean ground beef
2 carrots, diced
1 celery stalk, diced
1 (28-ounce) can diced tomatoes
4 cups beef broth
1/4 teaspoon brown sugar
1/4 teaspoon salt
1/4 teaspoon pepper
1 cup alphabet pasta, uncooked

1. In a large skillet, brown the meat over medium-high heat; drain off fat and transfer the meat to the slow cooker.
2. Add the carrots, celery, tomatoes, broth, brown sugar, salt, and pepper to the slow cooker.
3. Cook on LOW for 4 to 6 hours, or on HIGH for 2 to 3 hours.
4. Add the pasta, and cook for an additional 30 minutes on HIGH.

 Tip: If you have frozen peas or corn on hand, thaw a handful or so and add with the pasta. Any type of small pasta can be used in this recipe—it won't change the flavor of the soup, just the name!

Tangy Tomato Soup with Baby Meatballs

QuickEase

Tiny meatballs create a big splash in this tomato and herb concoction. Choose the ripest tomatoes you can find—if you're lucky, right from the garden.

Serves 6

6 large ripe tomatoes, chopped
1 onion, chopped
1 carrot, chopped
1 tablespoon flour
4 cups chicken broth
2 bay leaves
1 tablespoon dried basil

$1/2$ teaspoon salt
$1/2$ teaspoon dried tarragon
$1/2$ pound ground beef
1 cup bread crumbs
1 egg
$1/4$ teaspoon nutmeg

1. Combine the tomatoes, onion, and carrot in the slow cooker.
2. Sprinkle with the flour, and add the broth, bay leaves, basil, salt, and tarragon.
3. In a bowl, combine the beef, bread crumbs, egg, and nutmeg, and form into small balls.
4. Add the meatballs to the slow cooker.
5. Cook on LOW for 6 to 8 hours, or on HIGH for 3 to 4 hours.
6. Discard the bay leaves before serving.

 Tip: Make the meatballs the night before, refrigerate, and add to assembled ingredients the next morning before leaving for work.

Tropical Pepper Pot

33 Minutes

On a cold winter night when sunshine and beach sand are almost unimaginable, this spicy cauldron of flavors is sure to take the chill from your bones.

Serves 8

1½ pounds stewing beef
¼ pound salt pork, diced
1 tablespoon oil
2 cloves garlic, minced
1 onion, chopped
1 green pepper, chopped
½ teaspoon pepper

3 sweet potatoes, cubed
1 tomato, chopped
3 cups fresh spinach, stems removed
1 cup kale, chopped
1 teaspoon hot pepper sauce
8 cups water

1. In a large skillet, brown the beef and salt pork in oil over medium-high heat.
2. Add garlic, onion, green pepper, and pepper, and cook over medium-high heat for an additional 3 minutes.
3. Transfer the mixture to the slow cooker, and add the potatoes, tomatoes, spinach, kale, hot pepper sauce, and water.
4. Cook on **LOW** for 8 to 10 hours, or on **HIGH** for 4 to 5 hours.

 Tip: If kale is not available, use Swiss chard or extra spinach.

Pork and Pepper Pot

QuickEase

*A delightful hot-and-sour soup that makes a fabulous
first impression at your next dinner party.*

Serves 6

2 pork chops, boneless, diced
1 tablespoon sherry
1 tablespoon rice vinegar
1 tablespoon soy sauce
$1/2$ teaspoon pepper
1 green pepper, diced
1 green onion, thinly sliced
5 cups chicken broth
$1/3$ cup uncooked rice

1. Combine all the ingredients *except* the rice
   in the slow cooker.
2. Cook on **LOW** for 5 to 6 hours, or on
   HIGH for $2^{1}/2$ to 3 hours.
3. Stir in the rice, and cook for an additional
   45 minutes on **HIGH**.

 Tip: Rice vinegar is less acidic and milder
in taste than regular vinegar. It is sometimes called rice wine vinegar but is not
the same thing as rice wine, so when
purchasing, read the label carefully!

First Impressions

A friend of mine is big on garage
sales, so when she was invited to
her new boyfriend's parents' home
for the first time, she set aside an
entire weekend to find the perfect
hostess gift. After much searching,
she came upon a lovely old foot-
stool with dainty wooden legs and a
beautiful needlepoint design. She
couldn't believe how little the owner
was asking—some people don't recognize beauty even when it's right
under their nose! Once my friend
got the treasure home, she decided
not to refinish it; a few scratches
and the slightly worn-out fabric
were part of the stool's charm. On
the big day, her boyfriend picked her
up. Everything was great until he
drove into a familiar neighborhood.
Her heart sank when he pulled into
the driveway from which she'd
bought the stool.

Red Kidney Bean Soup

33 Minutes

Beans, vegetables, and pork with a hint of cloves combine to make a thick, creamy soup without the added calories of cream.

Serves 8
3 pork chops, boneless, cubed
2 (19-ounce) cans red kidney beans, rinsed and drained
2 leeks, chopped (white part only)
2 celery stalks, chopped
1 carrot, chopped
1 tomato, chopped
3 cloves, whole
1 tablespoon soy sauce
1 teaspoon salt
1/2 teaspoon pepper
3 cups chicken broth
1 envelope dried chicken noodle soup mix

1. Combine all the ingredients in the slow cooker.
2. Cook on **LOW** for 8 to 10 hours, or on **HIGH** for 4 to 5 hours.
3. Transfer soup to blender or food processor, and purée in batches until smooth.
4. Return to the slow cooker, and cook for an additional 30 minutes on **HIGH**.

 Tip: Before puréeing, remove a handful of beans and leave them whole for garnish.

Carrot and Bacon Soup

33 Minutes

Bacon adds a smoky depth to the refreshing taste of carrots.
Let loose your artistic flair with a dollop of sour cream.

Serves 6

6 slices bacon
5 carrots, diced
4 potatoes, diced
1 large onion,
   chopped
½ teaspoon dried basil
6 cups chicken broth
Sour cream
   (optional)

1. Combine all the ingredients *except* the sour cream in the slow cooker.
2. Cook on LOW for 8 to 10 hours, or on HIGH for 4 to 5 hours.
3. Transfer to a blender or food processor, and purée in batches until smooth.
4. Return to the slow cooker, and cook for an additional 30 minutes on HIGH; serve with sour cream.

Tip: If you're watching your diet, cook bacon until crispy, transfer 1 tablespoon bacon drippings to slow cooker, and serve bacon crumbled on the side.

Smoked Golden Pea Soup

QuickEase

*Tender chunks of smoked pork hock add flavor and depth
to a thick sea of yellow split peas, veggies, and spices.*

Serves 8

1 pound smoked pork hock

$^1/2$ pound dried yellow split peas, rinsed

2 celery stalks, finely chopped

1 onion, chopped

1 carrot, diced

2 teaspoons beef bouillon granules

1 bay leaf

$^1/2$ teaspoon pepper

$^1/4$ teaspoon ground cloves

6 cups water

1. Combine all the ingredients in the slow cooker.
2. Cook on LOW for 8 to 10 hours, or on HIGH for 4 to 5 hours.
3. Discard bay leaf, and remove pork hocks.
4. Cut the meat from the bone into bite-size cubes, return to slow cooker, and serve.

 Tip: This soup is so filling it can easily be served as a main course with salad and bread.

A Letter I'd Love to Write

Dear Fellow Driver,

Sorry for making you arrive at your destination 5 seconds later than you planned. I'm the horrible person who was in front of you at the stoplight, and failed to go the instant the light turned green. Shame on me for daydreaming about where I would get the money for my daughter's braces. Anyway, I wanted to say thanks for blowing your horn, not just a light tap, but really *leaning* on it. Thanks for going around me. And thanks for showing me your middle finger. My daughter with the crooked teeth was in the backseat and she enjoyed learning the innovative ways adults communicate. Once you blasted past, I noticed you turned left into the furniture store. Whew, now I understand why you were in such a hurry. I know me—when I need a couch, I need one *now*.

Sincerely,
Silly Me

Cabbage Soup with Pork Meatballs

QuickEase

*A hearty, economical soup sure to be a hit with those
who love cooked cabbage. Here, pork penetrates
the broth, adding rich bites of flavor.*

Serves 8
Half head cabbage, roughly chopped
2 potatoes, diced
1 carrot, grated
1 tablespoon brown sugar
$1/2$ teaspoon pepper
$1/2$ teaspoon salt
8 cups chicken broth
$1/4$ pound ground pork

1. Combine all the ingredients *except* the pork in the slow cooker.
2. Cook on LOW for 6 to 8 hours, or on HIGH for 3 to 4 hours.
3. Form the pork into tiny meatballs.
4. Add the meatballs to the slow cooker, and cook for an additional 1 hour on LOW.

 Tip: To add a bit of kick to the pork, mix in some freshly ground black pepper before forming it into balls.

Healing Chicken Soup

QuickEase

A time-honored favorite with healing powers to calm coughs, soothe throats, and settle the queasiest tummy. If made with love, 1 bowlful can mend a broken heart.

Serves 8

8 cups chicken broth
2 cups cubed cooked chicken
3 carrots, sliced
2 celery stalks, sliced
$1/4$ teaspoon dried basil
$1/4$ teaspoon salt
$1/4$ teaspoon pepper
1 cup small pasta, uncooked

1. Combine the broth, chicken, carrots, celery, basil, salt, and pepper in the slow cooker.
2. Cook on LOW for 6 to 8 hours, or on HIGH for 3 to 4 hours.
3. Add the pasta, and cook for an additional 30 minutes on HIGH.

 Tip: To add an extra dimension to this soup, form $1/3$ pound lean ground beef into tiny meatballs and add with pasta.

Some Grandmotherly Advice

A few years ago I had the flu so bad I couldn't get out of bed. The kids were little, so Hubby had to take over. One morning, my grandmother called to check in. By then, I'd been sick a few days and was just starting to feel better.

"I'm not too bad, Nanny," I chirped, "In fact, I'm thinking of getting up for a bit, maybe throwing in a load of laundry."

Nanny gasped.

"Are ya crazy? Here's what I know about men: they'll look after you for as long as you're bedridden, but won't lift a finger once they see your feet hit the floor."

Something in her tone made my toes curl.

"Geez. I'm not feeling so hot after all."

"Of course you're not," she sympathized. "Now put that husband of yours on the phone so I can give him my recipe for chicken soup."

Chinese Chicken Soup

QuickEase

*Containing no pasta, rice, or potatoes, this delicious,
light soup makes an excellent first course.*

Serves 6
6 cups chicken broth
2 cups shredded cooked chicken
1 cup thinly sliced mushrooms
3 green onions, thinly sliced (white part only)
3 tablespoons soy sauce
1/4 teaspoon salt
1/4 teaspoon pepper
1 egg

1. Combine all the ingredients *except* the egg in the slow
   cooker.
2. Cook on LOW for 3 to 4 hours, or on HIGH for 1 1/2 to
   2 hours.
3. Turn to HIGH.
4. Beat the egg until frothy, and slowly add it to the slow
   cooker in a steady stream, whisking soup constantly.
5. Cook for an additional 5 minutes, and serve immediately.

 Tip: Rather than discarding the green part of the
onions, chop them up and sprinkle into soup for
garnish.

Tex-Mex Chicken Soup

WhamBam

If nothing else turns out right today, not to worry, this lip-smacking spicy soup will. An easy choice for a busy day.

Serves 6

6 cups chicken broth
2 cups shredded cooked chicken
2 cups bottled chunky mild salsa

1. Combine all the ingredients in the slow cooker.
2. Cook on **LOW** for 2 to 4 hours, or on **HIGH** for 1 to 2 hours.

Tip: This soup is excellent served with tortilla chips and shredded Cheddar or Monterey jack cheese.

School Daze

It's that dreadful time of the year again: Parent/Teacher Interview. One minute you're a confident mother with a list of issues to address, the next you're a banished child waiting in the hallway. When the classroom door finally opens, a couple emerges clinging to each other for support. You pray for a fire drill. Once inside, the teacher leads you to a little table with 2 little chairs. She gracefully takes a seat; you squat . . . and land with a plunk. She hands you a piece of artwork. You pray there's been some mistake. But no, your kid's signature is in the corner. The e is backward; worse, there's no e in his name! The teacher is talking, but you can't focus on her words. She asks if you have questions, but you can't remember what they are! Finally, you're dismissed. Dazed and confused, you stumble out of the classroom . . . striking fear into the hearts of those waiting in the hallway.

Mulligatawny

33 Minutes

A spicy Indian soup chock-full of chicken, lentils, and rice.
Coconut milk adds a splash of creamy sweetness.

Serves 8

1 pound boneless, skinless
   chicken thighs, cubed
2 onions, diced
2 cloves garlic, minced
1 tablespoon oil
1 celery stalk, diced
1/2 cup green lentils, rinsed
1 tablespoon dried parsley
1 teaspoon ground coriander

1/2 teaspoon turmeric
1/2 teaspoon ground ginger
1/2 teaspoon ground cumin
1/2 teaspoon cayenne
6 cups chicken broth
1 bay leaf
1 apple, peeled and diced
1 cup coconut milk
3 cups cooked rice

1. In a large skillet, brown the chicken, onions, and garlic lightly in oil over medium-high heat.
2. Stir in the celery, lentils, parsley, coriander, turmeric, ginger, cumin, cayenne, and 1 cup of the broth; cook over medium-high heat for an additional 3 minutes.
3. Transfer the mixture to the slow cooker.
4. Add the remaining broth, bay leaf, and apple to the slow cooker.
5. Cook on LOW for 6 to 8 hours, or on HIGH for 3 to 4 hours.
6. Discard the bay leaf, stir in the coconut milk, and cook for an additional 30 minutes on LOW. Ladle over bowls of cooked rice.

 Tip: Dried lentils do not have to be presoaked; however, pick through them and discard any stones or foreign matter you may find.

Harira

33 Minutes

A Muslim soup traditionally served after sunset during the month of Ramadan. Here, lamb, lentils, chickpeas, and tomatoes unite in a spicy chicken broth.

Serves 10

2 lamb chops, cubed
1 onion, chopped
1 tablespoon oil
$^1/_2$ cup green lentils, rinsed
1 (19-ounce) can chickpeas,
    rinsed and drained
2 tomatoes, chopped
2 teaspoons dried parsley
1 teaspoon cinnamon

$^1/_2$ teaspoon ground ginger
$^1/_2$ teaspoon pepper
$^1/_4$ teaspoon salt
$^1/_4$ teaspoon saffron
8 cups chicken broth
2 tablespoons chopped cilantro
1 tablespoon lemon juice
harissa

1. In a large skillet, brown the lamb cubes and onion in oil over medium-high heat.
2. Add the lentils, chickpeas, tomatoes, parsley, cinnamon, ginger, pepper, salt, and saffron; cook over medium-high heat for 3 minutes, stirring constantly.
3. Transfer the mixture to the slow cooker, and add the broth.
4. Cook on **LOW** for 8 to 10 hours, or on **HIGH** for 4 to 5 hours.
5. Add the cilantro and lemon juice, and serve with harissa on the side.

Tip: Harissa is a hot condiment available in Middle Eastern food stores; if unavailable, use sambal oelek, or omit.

Roasted Tomato and Garlic Soup

33 Minutes

*Makes a gourmazing first impression. Roasted cloves of garlic
lend a smoky sweetness to this hip and healthful soup. Gourmazing stuff.*

Serves 6

10 ripe plum toma-
   toes, halved
1 onion, quartered
2 tablespoons olive oil
1/2 teaspoon pepper

1/4 teaspoon salt
2 heads garlic, cloves
   separated, unpeeled
3 cups chicken *or*
   vegetable broth

2 tablespoons tomato paste
1 bay leaf
1/4 teaspoon dried thyme
1 teaspoon lemon juice
1/2 teaspoon brown sugar

1. Preheat oven to 425°. In a large bowl, combine the tomatoes, onion, olive oil, pepper, and salt.
2. Transfer to baking sheet, placing tomatoes cut-side down.
3. Add the garlic cloves, and bake vegetables for 20 minutes.
4. Once cool enough to handle, squeeze garlic cloves out of their skins and add to slow cooker, along with tomato mixture.
5. Stir the broth, tomato paste, bay leaf, and thyme into the slow cooker.
6. Cook on LOW for 4 to 6 hours, or on HIGH for 2 to 3 hours.
7. Discard the bay leaf, and transfer the soup to a blender or food processor; purée in batches until smooth.
8. Return mixture to the slow cooker, stir in the lemon juice and brown sugar, and serve.

 Tip: Although this soup requires some effort preparing, you can make up for lost time by serving it as a main course with a simple tossed salad and a basket of warm crusty bread.

Minestrone

QuickEase

Beans, pasta, spices, and chopped vegetables star in this comforting Italian classic. Top with heaps of freshly grated Parmesan and freshly ground pepper.

Serves 10

2 cups Swiss chard, chopped
2 cloves garlic, minced
1 onion, chopped
1 carrot, chopped
1 celery stalk
1 zucchini, chopped
1 teaspoon dried basil
$1/2$ teaspoon pepper
6 cups chicken broth
1 (28-ounce) can plum tomatoes, broken up
1 (19-ounce) can white kidney beans, rinsed and drained
$1/2$ cup small pasta, uncooked

1. Combine all the ingredients *except* the pasta in the slow cooker.
2. Cook on LOW for 4 to 6 hours, or on HIGH for 2 to 3 hours.
3. Add the pasta, and cook for an additional 30 minutes on HIGH.

 Tip: Feel free to use other vegetables, such as cabbage, string beans, and parsnips.

Smoked Turkey and Lentil Soup

QuickEase

Smoked turkey, lentils, and veggies contribute their flavors to create homemade goodness spiked with just a dash of cayenne.

Serves 8

1 pound smoked turkey drumstick
2 carrots, sliced
1 leek, chopped (white part only)
1 celery stalk, diced
1 cup green lentils, rinsed
1 bay leaf
1/2 teaspoon salt
1/4 teaspoon pepper
1/4 teaspoon cayenne
6 cups water

1. Combine all the ingredients in the slow cooker.
2. Cook on LOW for 8 to 10 hours, or on HIGH for 4 to 5 hours.
3. Discard the bay leaf, and remove the turkey drumstick.
4. Debone the turkey, chop the meat, and return it to the slow cooker; serve.

 Tip: Smoked turkey parts are available in many supermarkets.

Which Craft?

There are only 2 types of women in this world: those who are good at crafts and those who are not. You can tell which category a woman falls into the moment you walk through her front door.

1. Crafters' homes are messy. Your elbows will stick to the kitchen table, and you'll leave with something stuck to your butt. Noncrafters, on the other hand, prefer more organized chaos; there are only shopping bags and empty boxes to trip over.
2. Crafters are packed to the rafters with wreaths, knickknacks, and hand-painted wooden signs. Noncrafters have the same stuff, only less, and it's more symmetrical.
3. Crafters are always home. Yes, that's a glue-gun in her pocket *and* she's happy to see you. Noncrafters are never in. Forever out shopping, they spend their lives at one-of-a-kind craft shows forking out big bucks for anything that looks homemade.

Coconut Curry Red Lentil Soup

QuickEase

When you can't decide what to make, choose this magnificently spiced soup in which red lentils lose their shape in a creamy coconut concoction.

Serves 6

1½ cups red lentils, rinsed
1 onion, diced
3 cups chicken *or* vegetable broth
1½ cups coconut milk
2 teaspoons curry powder
1 teaspoon ground ginger
¼ teaspoon garlic powder

1. Combine all the ingredients in the slow cooker.
2. Cook on LOW for 6 to 8 hours, or on HIGH for 3 to 4 hours.

 Tip: Among the oldest cultivated foods in the world, lentils are a member of the legume family. They are low calorie, low-fat, and low in price, but absolutely packed with nutrients!

Decisions, Decisions

Red lentils are actually orange and turn yellow when they're cooked. And my husband thinks I'm indecisive! Why, just the other day when I was trying to choose a paint color, he got all red in the head when I made him hold each little chip against the wall.

"Just pick one," he snapped. "Hell, it's only paint."

Or the time I was trying to decide on a new hairstyle. He flipped his lid when I made him watch as I held dozens of magazine photos next to my face.

"Just pick one," he snapped. "Hell, it's only hair."

Hmph. I don't think I'm going to involve him in the decision-making process anymore. Just imagine how delighted he'll be when I pull into the driveway in a brand-new car that screams CHICK-mobile.

"I just picked one," I'll tell him. "Hell, it's only money."

Vegetable Soup Creole

Enjoy Louisiana's favorite combo—celery, onions, and green peppers—in this spicy vegetarian first course.

Serves 6

2 celery stalks, diced
1 green pepper, chopped
1 onion, chopped
1 (28-ounce) can tomatoes,
    broken up
2 tablespoons chipotle
    pepper sauce

1 bay leaf
1/2 teaspoon dried parsley
1/4 teaspoon dried thyme
1/4 teaspoon salt
1/4 teaspoon pepper
6 cups vegetable broth
3 cups cooked rice

1. Combine all the ingredients *except* the rice in the slow cooker.
2. Cook on LOW for 6 to 8 hours, or on HIGH for 3 to 4 hours.
3. Ladle into bowls of rice.

 Tip: Chipotle pepper sauce adds a smoky flavor, but you may substitute any pepper sauce as long as you adjust the quantity according to its heat and your taste buds!

Mellow Yellow Corn Soup with Saffron

QuickEase

A little saffron goes a long way in flavoring this beautiful monochromatic soup of corn and yellow peppers in a mild golden broth.

Serves 4

2 cups frozen corn kernels
1 sweet yellow pepper, chopped
1 large potato, cubed
1 onion, chopped
1 teaspoon butter
1/2 teaspoon saffron threads
1/4 teaspoon white pepper
1/4 teaspoon salt
3 cups chicken *or* vegetable broth

1. Combine all the ingredients in the slow cooker.
2. Cook on **LOW** for 4 to 6 hours, or on **HIGH** for 2 to 3 hours.

 Tip: Saffron is a very expensive spice made from the stamens of the crocus flower. Buy it in threads, and store in a cool (safe!) place, not too close to the stove.

Your Neighbor's Point of View

These days there are so many wonderful colors of house paint to choose from with lovely names such as Aspen Mist, Swan's Song, and Mellow Yellow. If you're painting the interior of your home, go wild—after all, you're the one who has to look at it all day. Of course, the same cannot be said for the exterior. No, when you paint your garage door Purple Passion, you really only see it when you pull in and out of your driveway. I, on the other hand, get the shock of my life every time I glance out my living room window or open my front door. Can you imagine what would happen if everyone on the street decided to make a statement with a paintbrush? Why, the value of the neighborhood would drop to that of a box of crayons! So please, go subtle. Bland Beige is always in.

Cream of Asparagus Soup Amandine

33 Minutes

*Almonds and asparagus make the "A" list in this gorgeous
green soup that tastes like the first day of spring.*

Serves 6
1 pound asparagus, trimmed, chopped
$1/2$ cup ground almonds
1 leek, sliced (white part only)
1 potato, cubed
1 tablespoon butter
$1/4$ teaspoon pepper
4 cups chicken *or* vegetable broth
$1/2$ cup cream

1. Combine all the ingredients *except* the cream in the slow cooker.
2. Cook on LOW for 6 to 8 hours, or on HIGH for 3 to 4 hours.
3. Transfer to a blender or food processor, and purée in batches until smooth.
4. Return the mixture to the slow cooker, add the cream, and cook for an additional 30 minutes on LOW.

Tip: Ground almonds are available in bulk food stores and larger supermarkets. To grind your own, use a clean coffee grinder or a food processor. Be careful not to grind too much or you'll end up with paste! This soup can be made lighter by omitting the ground almonds and/or using milk instead of cream.

Cream of Wild Mushroom Soup

33 Minutes

*Ordinary white mushrooms blend with their more exotic counterparts
to create a silky soup with a wild and woodsy flavor.*

Serves 6

2 cups chopped mushrooms	1 tablespoon sherry
2 cups chopped assorted wild mushrooms	1/4 teaspoon dried marjoram
	1/4 teaspoon pepper
1 onion, chopped	4 cups chicken broth
1 large potato, cubed	1/2 cup cream

1. Combine all the ingredients *except* the cream in the slow cooker.
2. Cook on LOW for 6 to 8 hours, or on HIGH for 3 to 4 hours.
3. Transfer to a blender or food processor, and purée in batches until smooth.
4. Return the mixture to the slow cooker, add the cream, and cook for an additional 30 minutes on LOW.

 Tip: Try a blend of mushrooms such as portobello, shiitake, and oyster. To clean, wipe gently with a soft brush or damp cloth. If you're using shiitake or portobello mushrooms, tear off and discard the woody stems.

Cream of Sweet Potato Soup

33 Minutes

*Looks like a sunset; tastes like heaven. Let this glowing soup
be the sweetest thing at the table . . . next to you.*

Serves 6

4 large sweet potatoes, cubed
1 onion, chopped
2 pieces crystallized ginger, chopped
1 1/2 teaspoons butter
3 cups chicken *or* vegetable broth
3/4 cup cream

1. Combine all the ingredients *except* the cream in the slow cooker.
2. Cook on LOW for 8 to 10 hours, or on HIGH for 4 to 5 hours.
3. Transfer to a blender or food processor, and purée in batches until smooth.
4. Return the mixture to the slow cooker, add the cream, and cook for an additional 30 minutes on LOW.

 Tip: Sprinkle some brown sugar in each bowl for over-the-top sweetness appeal.

Sweet Beginnings . . .

Men are wonderful at the beginning of relationships. They're kind, complimentary, and so romantic. From all that I've heard (and a few I've experienced), this is my favorite how-sweet-it-was story. My girlfriend was bored to tears, enduring a 5-hour, stop-at-every-small-town train-ride home. She had been away for only a few days, but was anxious to get back to her new lover. About 100 miles or so outside of her hometown, the train stopped to let passengers on and off. For something to do, she watched them board. Suddenly, she saw a tall, dark, handsome man walking up the aisle toward her. She held her breath. He held her gaze . . . and a single red rose. She blinked. Yes, it was her lover! Unable to bear another few hours without her, he had hitched a ride in her direction so he could intercept the train. *Gaaawwwd.*

Potato-Leek Soup

Proof that potatoes and leeks are meant for each other lies in this rich, creamy soup. Delicate yet hearty, it will satisfy discerning taste buds and demanding appetites alike.

Serves 6

5 potatoes, cubed
3 leeks, thinly sliced (white part only)
1 onion, finely chopped
$1/4$ teaspoon pepper
$1/4$ teaspoon salt
4 cups chicken *or* vegetable broth
$2/3$ cup cream

1. Combine all the ingredients *except* the cream in the slow cooker.
2. Cook on LOW for 8 to 10 hours, or on HIGH for 4 to 5 hours.
3. Using a potato masher, smash the potatoes a few times to break them up a bit.
4. Add the cream, and cook for an additional 30 minutes on LOW.

 Tip: The leek is a member of the onion family but has a far milder taste. When purchasing, look for ones with white bulbs and fresh green tops. *To clean:* Cut off roots and green part. Cut white part in half lengthwise. Rinse halves under cold running water, making sure you remove all the dirt trapped between the layers.

Bouillabaisse

33 Minutes

*Treat guests to a Poseidon adventure with schools of fish
and seafood in a tomato and wine-broth sea.*

Serves 8

1 onion, chopped
1 celery stalk, chopped
1 leek, chopped (white part only)
1 carrot, thinly sliced
2 cloves garlic, minced
3 tablespoons oil
1 teaspoon dried parsley
1/2 teaspoon dried thyme
1/2 teaspoon pepper
1/4 teaspoon salt

1/8 teaspoon cayenne
1 bay leaf
1 (28-ounce) can tomatoes
4 cups water
1/2 cup dry white wine
1 1/2 pounds fish fillets, cut into
    bite-size pieces
1 cup raw shrimp, peeled and
    deveined
1 cup scallops

1. In a large skillet, cook the onion, celery, leek, carrot, and garlic in oil over medium-high heat for 3 minutes.
2. Add the parsley, thyme, pepper, salt, cayenne, bay leaf, and tomatoes; bring to a boil.
3. Transfer the mixture to the slow cooker, and add the water and wine.
4. Cook on LOW for 6 to 8 hours, or on HIGH for 3 to 4 hours.
5. Add the fish and shrimp, and cook for an additional 15 minutes.
6. Discard the bay leaf, add the scallops, and cook for an additional 10 minutes.

Tip: White fish—such as haddock, cod, red snapper, and bass—works best in this recipe.

Easy Crab Bisque

WhamBam

Taking only minutes to prepare, this satisfying bisque provides just enough strength to get you through a seemingly endless day.

Serves 4

2 (10-ounce) cans condensed cream of chicken soup

2 (4-ounce) cans crabmeat, undrained

$1^3/_4$ cups milk

1. Combine the soup and crabmeat in the slow cooker.
2. Cook on LOW for 2 hours.
3. Stir in the milk, and cook for an additional 30 minutes on LOW.

Tip: Served with salt and plenty of pepper, the taste of crab is surprisingly prominent in this soup and sure to please seafood enthusiasts.

At the End of the Day . . .

Dear Mommy,

We had fun tonight while you were out. Daddy said I could put marshmallows in my soup for dinner but he forgot to make the soup. Anyway, he said to leave you a note about everything I need for school tomorrow so you won't be a crab in the morning. Please sign my permission form, math test, and the thing saying you'll help me read. I need cardboard for my dinosaur project, and a costume cuz it's Pioneer Day. I need brownies for the bake sale and Mrs. Baldwin says they have to be homemade. She wants to know if you'll work at the sale cuz you signed that volunteer thing at the beginning of the year and you haven't done anything yet. Mr. Antonio says if I don't have non-marking shoes by Monday I'll get kicked out of gym. And don't forget to pick me up after school cuz it's our weekend to bring home Mr. Ears. Thanks, Mom.

Love, Trevor

New Brunswick Seafood Chowder

QuickEase

Enjoy a taste of Eastern Canada with this thick, down-home chowder. An ocean of compliments awaits you.

Serves 8

4 potatoes, diced
1 onion, chopped
1 tablespoon butter
1/4 cup dry white wine
2 (5-ounce) cans clams, undrained
2 cups milk
1 (13-ounce) can evaporated milk
1/2 pound haddock
1 cup cooked shrimp
1/2 cup scallops
2 cups instant garlic-flavored mashed potato flakes

1. Combine the potatoes, onion, butter, wine, and clams with juice in the slow cooker.
2. Cook on LOW for 6 to 8 hours, or on HIGH for 3 to 4 hours.
3. Add the milk, evaporated milk, haddock, and shrimp; cook for an additional 20 minutes.
4. Stir in the scallops and potato flakes, and cook for an additional 10 minutes.

 Tip: Don't hesitate to try your favorite types of fish and seafood.

Manhattan Clam Chowder

33 Minutes

A spicy tomato-based chowder for seafood lovers with big-city tastes. Serve steaming hot with crusty rolls and salad.

Serves 6

4 slices bacon, chopped
3 potatoes, diced
2 celery stalks, diced
1 onion, diced
1 clove garlic, minced
1 tablespoon lemon juice
1 teaspoon pepper

1 bay leaf
1 (28-ounce) can diced
   tomatoes
2 (5-ounce) cans clams,
   undrained
1 cup chicken broth
1/8 teaspoon hot pepper sauce

1. Cook the bacon until it is crisp, drain, and transfer to the slow cooker.
2. Combine the potatoes, celery, onion, garlic, lemon juice, pepper, bay leaf, tomatoes, clams with juice, and broth in the slow cooker.
3. Cook on LOW for 6 to 8 hours, or on HIGH for 3 to 4 hours.
4. Discard the bay leaf and add the hot pepper sauce just before serving.

 Tip: For larger crowds, this recipe can easily be doubled.

The Perfect Spread— Main Courses

recipe list continued on following page

73

✱ Pork

recipe list continued on following page

✱ Fish and Seafood

✱ Vegetarian

Three hundred and sixty-five days a year you have to worry about making dinner. If you order in or eat out twice a month, that knocks it down to 341. Minus 1 or 2 weeks' holidaying where someone else feeds you (ideally a resort—but likely your mother-in-law's), and you're still hovering around the three hundred and something mark. Girl, no wonder you're stressed. But chill. This is where slow cookers really kick in.

From now on, when you're wondering what to have for dinner, visions of pizza and rotisserie chickens will be replaced with the likes of PersuAsian Beef, Pork Roast in Red Pepper Jelly Sauce, Poached Chicken Velouté, and Spicy Chickpea Casserole with Quinoa. You'll not only know what these dishes are; you'll actually know how to prepare them. And, if you practice wrapping your tongue around such phrases as *Darling, let's indulge in a little Cranberry Beef Fling* or *Gotta fly, my Golden Cornish Hens on a Bed of Caramelized Onions are roosting,* in no time you'll master the impressive art of recipe name-dropping, a simple trick chefs use to enhance their reputation as gourmets. Allow me to present a few other tips:

1. **Buy a pepper mill.** Imagine a waiter offering you pepper and whipping out a giant shaker. It's not going to happen because any chef worth her salt knows freshly cracked peppercorns add tremendous flavor to a meal. So purchase a pepper mill and place it in full view on your kitchen table. It's a phallic phenomenon that's sure to delight.

2. **Dump your spices.** A dead-giveaway of a rookie chef is a spice-rack with jars filled to the brim. It simply screams,

I bought this prefilled cuz it looks so pretty, but I've never used anything but the parsley. Contrary to popular belief, dried herbs do not last forever and God only knows how long they've sat in those jars. Throw them out, and every time you visit the supermarket's bulk food section, purchase a little bit of this and a little bit of that until your rack features as many levels as an equalizer.

3. **Open your infusions.** You know that beautifully shaped jar you have containing oil with some seaweedlike substance seemingly growing inside? It's not merely a decoration; it's flavor-infused oil for use in cooking! That gunky wax topping collecting dust is meant to be removed! And the cap beneath it comes off so you can get at the liquid! Even if you never cook with the stuff, at least open the bloody thing and empty some out so guests will think you do.

Warning: These tips will make people think you're a chef. However, mastering a main course is what separates the wonder women from the wannabes, so girl, step up to the plate.

Thai Beef Curry

QuickEase

Red curry paste ignites tender strips of beef and red peppers.
Lusty stuff—do get rid of the kids!

Serves 4

1¹/₂ pounds round steak, cut into
  strips
1 red pepper, cut into strips
1¹/₂ cups coconut milk
1 tablespoon red curry paste
1 tablespoon lime juice
1 teaspoon fish sauce *or* soy sauce

1. Place the steak and red pepper in
   the slow cooker.
2. In a bowl, mix together the coconut
   milk, red curry paste, lime juice,
   and fish sauce (*or* soy sauce); pour
   over the steak.
3. Cook on **LOW** for 6 to 8 hours, or
   on **HIGH** for 3 to 4 hours.

 Tip: Fish sauce is a thin, brown
liquid made from salted fish. It's
a Thai cooking staple. If you're
not fond of its strong taste, use
soy sauce instead.

The Parenthood Championships

Welcome to the 1st Annual Parenthood Championships, where parents across the nation compete to see who is run most ragged by their kids' afterschool activities. Our goal is to declare a clear winner, thus ceasing the constant one-upmanship exhibited wherever people meet, from water coolers to pool parties. The following formula will determine the champion:

(amount of kids you have) ×
(amount of activities they're involved in) ×
(total cost of activities) ×
(distance traveled to and from each activity) ×
(skill level at which each child participates)

This formula is fair to everyone. Those with multiple kids who are not gifted can achieve high points by loading them up with activities. Parents with only one kid can make up for lost points if Johnny is so advanced that he must be shipped outside your community to follow his Olympic dreams. Please note: We rely on your honesty, but reserve the right to cross-examine your kids.

PersuAsian Beef

At your next dinner party, you'll have no problem persuading guests to devour this pretty dish of Asian-spiced beef and bell peppers in a spicy soy sauce.

Serves 4

1 1/2 pounds round steak, cut into strips
1 red pepper, cut into strips
1 green pepper, cut into strips
2 green onions, chopped
1/4 teaspoon Chinese 5-spice
1/4 teaspoon black pepper
1/4 teaspoon cayenne
1/4 teaspoon garlic powder
1 tablespoon soy sauce
1/2 cup beef broth
2 tablespoons cornstarch
2 tablespoons water

1. Combine the steak, peppers, and onions in the slow cooker.
2. In a small bowl, mix together the Chinese 5-spice, pepper, cayenne, and garlic powder.
3. Sprinkle the spice mixture over the steak and peppers, and add the soy sauce and broth.
4. Cook on LOW for 6 to 8 hours, or on HIGH for 3 to 4 hours.
5. Mix together the cornstarch and water, add to the slow cooker, and cook for an additional 20 minutes on HIGH.

 Tip: Chinese 5-spice is a strong mixture of star anise, clove, fennel, cinnamon, and pepper, and is available in larger supermarkets and Asian markets.

Wine-and-Dine Beef

QuickEase

Common stewing beef soaks up some class thanks to hours spent in a creamy mushroom sauce imbued with good-quality dry red wine. Nice over rice or rice noodles.

Serves 4

1½ pounds stewing beef

2 onions, quartered

2 cloves garlic, minced

2 cups mushrooms, sliced

1 (10-ounce) can condensed cream of
    mushroom soup

½ cup dry red wine

2 tablespoons Worcestershire sauce

¼ teaspoon pepper

1. Combine all the ingredients in the slow cooker.
2. Cook on **LOW** for 8 to 10 hours, or on **HIGH** for 4 to 5 hours.

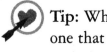 **Tip:** When cooking with wine, use one that is affordable enough to cook with, but good enough to drink.

My Dinner Party To-Do List

1. Get feminine hygiene stuff out of powder room vanity.
2. Stick blender, steamer, juicer, and waffle iron in basement.
3. Leave out slow cooker (of course); set out espresso machine (for show).
4. Take bills off fridge and replace with kids' best report cards.
5. Call Mary and tell her not to mention coat I put on layaway.
6. Call Mary and tell her not to mention last Friday night.
7. Move wrought-iron thing Mary gave me from spare room to dining room.
8. Buy recent CD. (Ask music store guy who's hip.)
9. Throw away Roasted Red Pepper Dip container so people think I made it.
10. Memorize today's headlines so people think I know what's going on.
11. Tell husband to act like we're all lovey-dovey.
12. Tell Mary to mention how lovey-dovey Hubby and I *always* are.

Cranberry Beef Fling

QuickEase

Cranberry abandons her traditional partner for a night to remember with beef.
Serve over rice for the visual drama of red wine and a stark-white tablecloth.

Serves 4

1½ pounds stewing beef

2 onions, chopped

1 clove garlic, minced

1 cup cranberry sauce (canned or
   homemade)

1 (19-ounce) can tomatoes, broken up

½ cup beef broth

¼ cup dry red wine

1 teaspoon dried basil

1 teaspoon dried oregano

½ teaspoon dried thyme

½ teaspoon pepper

1. Combine all the ingredients in the slow cooker.
2. Cook on **LOW** for 8 to 10 hours, or on **HIGH** for 4 to 5 hours.

 Tip: This recipe works well with any economical cut of steak trimmed of fat. To break up canned tomatoes, simply press them with a wooden spoon.

A Family Affair

It begins about 6 weeks before the actual event: a niggling feeling something bad is about to happen. Then, you get the call. It's a close relative—your sister, say—gleefully reminding you that it's your turn to host the family holiday meal.

"Didn't I have it last year?" you gasp.

"GONG!" she bellows, showing her age with an old game show impression. "You guys were at your in-laws."

"But didn't I have it the year before that?"

"GONG! I did. You brought the wine."

"But didn't Mom say from now on we're all going to a restaurant?"

"GONG! You argued it just wouldn't be the same."

"But, um, ah . . . so it's my turn?" A hope-filled pause. Then . . . "DINGDINGDINGDINGDING!"

Beef Stroganoff

QuickEase

A traditional Russian dish that blends tender strips of beef,
mushrooms, and onions in a soothing sour cream sauce.

Serves 4

1¹/₂ pounds round steak, cut into strips	¹/₄ teaspoon garlic powder
2 cups sliced mushrooms	¹/₄ teaspoon paprika
1 onion, chopped	¹/₄ teaspoon salt
1 tomato, chopped	¹/₄ teaspoon pepper
1¹/₂ cups beef broth	2 tablespoons flour
3 tablespoons sherry	3 tablespoons water
	1 cup sour cream

1. Combine the steak, mushrooms, onion, tomato, broth, sherry, garlic powder, paprika, salt, and pepper in the slow cooker.
2. Cook on LOW for 6 to 8 hours, or on HIGH for 3 to 4 hours.
3. Mix together the flour and water, and stir into the slow cooker.
4. Stir in the sour cream, and cook for an additional 20 minutes on HIGH.

 Tip: This recipe works well with any economical cut of steak or stewing beef, and is lovely over egg noodles.

Beef and Vegetable Stew

QuickEase

Tender chunks of beef amidst sturdy vegetables in a thick, rich gravy. Nothing fancy, but good. Really, really good.

Serves 4

1½ pounds stewing beef
3 potatoes, cubed
2 onions, quartered
2 carrots, thickly sliced
2 celery stalks, chopped
1 bay leaf
1 teaspoon Worcester-
   shire sauce

½ teaspoon pepper
¼ teaspoon salt
¼ teaspoon dried
   thyme
1¼ cups beef broth
3 tablespoons flour
¼ cup water

1. Combine all the ingredients *except* the flour and water in the slow cooker.
2. Cook on LOW for 8 to 10 hours, or on HIGH for 4 to 5 hours.
3. Discard the bay leaf, and mix together the flour and water.
4. Stir the flour mixture into the slow cooker, and cook for an additional 20 minutes on HIGH.

 Tip: Any root vegetable works well in this recipe, so don't hesitate to try others such as parsnips, turnips, or rutabaga.

Pardon My Garden

Just when you thought working, cooking, cleaning, and raising kids were enough, somebody invented the gardening craze. Now, you're expected to turn every square foot of unpaved soil into a vegetable crop, and adorn every railing, windowsill, and patio stone with flower-stuffed baskets and pots. Never mind you can't tell the difference between an annual and a perennial, a wildflower from a weed. Never mind you don't know what requires shade or sun, moist or dry soil. Never mind you're not good at Latin, and the English names sound the same. No, lucky for you, all the information you need to plant, grow, prune, and harvest each organism is written in symbols on a tiny tag. Of course, only a *moron* would plant the tag—real women are expected to remember. *Hmm*. Maybe it's time we switch to plastic flowers and just declare ourselves fakes.

Italian Beef Stew

QuickEase

Can stew be romantic? Sure. Set the table with a red-and-white-checkered tablecloth, turn on a little opera music, uncork a bottle of red wine . . . and have faith.

Serves 4

1½ pounds stewing beef
4 potatoes, cubed
2 onions, quartered
2 cloves garlic, minced
1 zucchini, quartered
   lengthwise and sliced
1 cup frozen lima beans
1 (28-ounce) can plum
   tomatoes, broken up

4 tablespoons tomato paste
2 tablespoons Italian seasoning
1 bay leaf
½ teaspoon salt
½ teaspoon pepper
¼ teaspoon red pepper flakes

1. Combine all the ingredients in the slow cooker.
2. Cook on LOW for 8 to 10 hours, or on HIGH for 4 to 5 hours.
3. Remove the bay leaf, and serve.

 Tip: Other Italian-type vegetables such as string beans and eggplant can be added. If Italian seasoning is unavailable, mix together equal parts of dried basil, oregano, and rosemary.

Steak and Orzo in Tomato-Oregano Sauce

QuickEase

If you're out gallivanting with the girls, leave your family this mild, simple dish in which everyday round steak is transformed into lick-your-plate pleasure.

Serves 4

1 1/2 pounds round steak, cubed
2 onions, chopped
1 cup tomato sauce
1 teaspoon dried oregano
1/2 teaspoon pepper
1/4 teaspoon salt
3/4 cups orzo, uncooked

1. Combine all the ingredients *except* the orzo in the slow cooker.
2. Cook on **LOW** for 6 to 8 hours, or on **HIGH** for 3 to 4 hours.
3. Stir in the orzo, and cook for an additional 10 minutes on **HIGH**.

 Tip: Orzo is a small, almond-shaped pasta that cooks very quickly.

Girls' Night Out Code of Conduct

It's fun to go wild and crazy once in a while, but there are a few rules to remember:

1. Never come out if you're not prepared to talk against your mate. Nothing kills a good male-bashing session like, "Gee, my husband's not like that."
2. Never launch into your latest childbirth story. The damn things are so contagious, in no time we'll all sound like the mother hens we are, instead of the hot chicks we're trying to be.
3. Never bring along some gorgeous friend we haven't met. Well, unless it's a guy.
4. Never arrange for your man to meet up with us during the evening. To you, he's a ride home; to us, he's a spy.
5. Never blab to your man about how one of us girls behaved. No matter how much you divulge, he still won't tell you what the guys did at the stag.

Share-It Steak and Sausage Pie

33 Minutes

Perfect for an informal Friday night family dinner.

Serves 4

6 frozen breakfast sausages

1 tablespoon oil

1 pound round steak, cut into
   bite-size pieces

1/4 cup flour

4 carrots, cut into bite-size pieces

1 onion, chopped

1 cup mushrooms, sliced

3/4 cup beef broth

1/2 teaspoon basil

1/2 teaspoon pepper

1/4 teaspoon salt

1 tablespoon cornstarch

1 tablespoon water

1 frozen puff pastry sheet, thawed

1. In a skillet, brown the sausages lightly in oil over medium-high heat.
2. Transfer the sausages to a cutting board, and slice. In a bag, shake the beef with the flour until well coated.
3. In the same skillet, lightly brown the steak pieces in the sausage drippings over medium-high heat. Transfer the steak to the slow cooker, along with the sausage, carrots, onions, mushrooms, broth, basil, pepper, and salt.
4. Cook on LOW for 6 to 8 hours, or on HIGH for 3 to 4 hours.
5. Mix together the cornstarch and water, stir into the slow cooker, and let cook for an additional 10 minutes on HIGH.
6. Transfer the steak and sausage mixture to a 9-inch deep-dish pie plate, cover with puff pastry according to package directions, and bake in 400° oven for 20 minutes or until golden.

 Tip: Thaw pastry overnight in the fridge or for a few hours on the counter.

Rouladen

QuickEase

Mushrooms and onions with surprising bites of dill pickle snugly rolled in bacon-lined beef cutlets. Precooked bacon contributes a subtle, smoky flavor.

Serves 4
6 round steak cutlets
1 tablespoon Dijon mustard
6 strips precooked bacon
1/2 cup canned mushrooms, finely chopped
1 large dill pickle, finely chopped
1 small onion, finely chopped
1/2 cup beef broth

1. Lay the cutlets in a row on a work surface, and spread mustard on one side of each.
2. Tear each bacon strip in half, and lay both pieces side by side on each cutlet.
3. In a bowl, mix together the mushrooms, pickle, and onion, and place some of the mixture on each cutlet.
4. Roll up the cutlets and secure with wooden toothpicks.
5. Transfer to the slow cooker, and pour broth over the top.
6. Cook on **LOW** for 6 to 8 hours, or on **HIGH** for 3 to 4 hours.

 Tip: Serve with hot juices on the side.

Black Bean Pot Roast

WhamBam

*After a long day at work, feel good knowing tender
roast beef with spicy black beans awaits you.*

Serves 6

3-pound beef pot roast

2 onions, sliced

2 (19-ounce) cans black bean soup

1. Place the roast in the slow cooker, cover
   with onions, and pour the soup over the top.
2. Cook on LOW for 8 to 10 hours, or on
   HIGH for 4 to 5 hours.
3. Remove the pot roast and keep warm.
4. Using a slotted spoon, remove the beans
   and serve on the side, along with the hot
   juices.

 Tip: Economical roasts such as blade,
rump, chuck, and cross-rib work best in
the slow cooker.

Doctor Feel-Good?

Why is it every time I set foot in a doctor's waiting room I begin to feel better? It's as if reading magazines for free rejuvenates my cells. On my last visit, by the time they called my name, I felt so good, I practically *danced* to the examination room. And after the nurse took my temperature, I'm sure she wrote FAKE on my chart. While waiting for the doctor, I had a chance to refocus on my aches and pains. But then I spotted a poster of human organs on the wall, and the more I studied it, the more I myself became a picture of health. By the time the doctor arrived, I could barely contain my joy. *How are you?* he asked gravely. *Never better!* I sang, raising my hand for a high-five.

Pot Roast in Mushrooms and Wine

WhamBam

For days when you've got a lot on your platter, add something simple such as roast beef bathed in plenty of gravy.

Serves 6

3-pound beef pot roast

1 (10-ounce) can condensed cream of mushroom soup

$^1/_2$ cup dry red wine

1. Place the roast in the slow cooker.
2. Mix together the soup and wine, and pour over the top of the roast.
3. Cook on **LOW** for 8 to 10 hours, or on **HIGH** for 4 to 5 hours.

 Tip: If you want to jazz up this dish, add a drained can of baby onions and/or sliced mushrooms to the soup and wine mixture. To get the most bang for your buck when purchasing a pot roast, look for an economical cut of beef that is bright red to deep red in color with some marbling, but not a lot of fat on the edges.

Could This Be on Your Fridge?

Weekly Dinner Schedule

Sunday—Pot Roast Night (Mommy makes nice roast with fresh veggies and gravy.)

Monday—Rotisserie Chicken Night (Mommy picks up chicken at deli. Kids set the table.)

Tuesday—Pizza Night (Remember to redeem Pepperoni Points.)

Wednesday—Leftovers Night (Mommy works late. Nuke whatever's in fridge. Smell first.)

Thursday—Frozen Waffles Night (Some people don't think of this as real food so DON'T EVEN THINK ABOUT inviting a friend over!)

Friday Night—Barbecue Night (Daddy's turn. Burgers. Whoop-dee-do.)

Saturday—Fend for Yourself Night (Mommy's grocery shopping so everybody take a turn with the can opener or wait till I bloody well get home, drag in all the grocery bags, unpack 'em, and rustle up something to eat even though I'm the one who'll be make making you all a nice pot roast dinner tomorrow!)

Brisket of Beef Esterházy

QuickEase

*In this Hungarian-inspired 1-pot pleasure, brisket of beef is
surrounded by roasted potatoes, turnips, carrots, and onions,
and served with a caper and sour cream gravy.*

Serves 6

3-pound beef brisket
3 potatoes, quartered
3 turnips, quartered
2 onions, quartered
2 carrots, thickly sliced
1 cup beef broth

¼ cup salt
¼ teaspoon pepper
1 cup sour cream
2 teaspoons capers, rinsed,
   chopped
1 teaspoon lemon juice

1. Place the brisket of beef in the slow cooker, and surround with
   potatoes, turnips, onions, and carrots.
2. Pour the beef broth over the brisket and vegetables, and sprinkle
   with salt and pepper.
3. Cook on LOW for 10 to 12 hours, or on HIGH for 5 to 6 hours.
4. Remove the beef and vegetables, and keep warm.
5. Add the sour cream, capers, and lemon juice to the juices in the
   slow cooker, stir to combine, and cook for an additional 10 minutes
   on LOW.

 Tip: If you like anchovies, chop a few and throw them in with
the capers and sour cream.

Pot Roast Provençale

QuickEase

In this specialty of France, beef lingers with freshly chopped tomatoes, onions,
and carrots in a mild broth destined to become a fabulous gravy.

Serves 6

3-pound beef pot roast
3 tomatoes, chopped
2 carrots, thickly sliced
1 onion, quartered
1 clove garlic, chopped

1 bay leaf
1 cup chicken broth
3 tablespoons flour
1/4 cup water

1. Place the roast in the slow cooker and surround with all the other ingredients *except* the flour and water.
2. Cook on LOW for 8 to 10 hours, or on HIGH for 4 to 5 hours.
3. Discard the bay leaf; remove the beef and vegetables, and keep warm.
4. Mix together the flour and water, whisk into the slow cooker, and cook for an additional 20 minutes on HIGH.

 Tip: If the roast won't fit in your slow cooker, cut it in half and stack them, with all the vegetables on the bottom.

Easy Corned Beef Brisket

WhamBam

*If only everything in life were this simple! The next time
you're away, leave this recipe for your hubby.*

Serves 6
3-pound corned beef brisket
5 whole cloves
Water to cover

1. Combine all the ingredients in the slow cooker.
2. Cook on **LOW** for 10 to 12 hours, or on **HIGH** for 5 to 6 hours.

 Tip: Corned beef is a beef brisket that has been cured with spices and brine. For an informal meal, serve corned beef thinly sliced with rye bread, mustard, and pickles so everyone can make their own deli-style sandwich. Ready-to-cook corned beef is typically more economical than corned beef purchased at the supermarket deli.

Out-of-Town Business Trips

A few days before a male colleague and I were going on a business trip, he made the mistake of telling me how eager he was to get away.

"I'm ready to go right now, Rebecca. Just point me toward the door."

"Really?" I grimaced. "Isn't that nice? All I have to do is a ton of laundry so my family has clean clothes to wear; a ton of groceries so they've all got their favorite things to eat; whip up a few casseroles so they won't order take-out every night; arrange for some other mother to drive them to and from soccer because my husband works late Tuesdays; cancel their dental appointments 'cause hell, who would take them? Pay the bills, put money on the credit cards, and arrange a cab to take me to the airport 'cause I won't have time to do park 'n fly!"

"Great," beamed my colleague. "See you on the plane."

Stuffed Green Peppers

QuickEase

Beef and rice in tomato sauce complete with an edible shell.
Round off the meal with soup and salad.

Serves 4
4 large green peppers
1 pound lean ground beef
1/2 cup rice, uncooked
1 onion, finely chopped
1/2 teaspoon pepper
1/4 teaspoon salt
1 (14-ounce) can tomato sauce

1. Cut off the tops of the peppers, and remove the membranes and seeds.
2. In a bowl, combine the beef, rice, onion, pepper, salt, and 1/4 cup of the tomato sauce.
3. Stuff the mixture into the peppers.
4. Transfer the peppers to the slow cooker, and pour the remaining tomato sauce over the top.
5. Cook on LOW for 6 to 8 hours, or on HIGH for 3 to 4 hours.

 Tip: Try ground pork, chicken, or turkey instead of beef. It's okay to stack the peppers, but make sure the ones at the bottom have tomato sauce over the top of them.

#41 Chili

33 Minutes

Next time you've got the gang for a football game, feed 'em chili with plenty of kick. Goes great with crusty rolls and plenty of cold beer.

Serves 6

2 pounds lean ground beef
1 teaspoon oil
2 cloves garlic, minced
1 onion, chopped
1 green pepper, chopped
2 tablespoons chili powder
1 tablespoon ground cumin
1/2 teaspoon pepper

1/2 teaspoon cayenne
1 (19-ounce) can red kidney
    beans, rinsed and drained
1 (28-ounce) can tomatoes,
    broken up
1 (5.5-ounce) can tomato paste
3/4 cup beef broth

1. In a large skillet, cook the beef over medium-high heat until no longer pink.
2. Drain off fat and transfer the meat to the slow cooker.
3. In a skillet, heat the oil on medium-high and cook the garlic, onion, green pepper, chili powder, cumin, pepper, and cayenne for 3 minutes.
4. Stir in the beans, tomatoes, tomato paste, and broth.
5. Transfer the mixture to the slow cooker.
6. Cook on **LOW** for 6 to 8 hours, or on **HIGH** for 3 to 4 hours.

 Tip: This recipe can easily be doubled if you have a big crowd and a large enough slow cooker.

Mama's Spaghetti Sauce and Meatballs

QuickEase

Who doesn't love a Saturday night meal of good ol' spaghetti and meatballs?
The secret to the sauce lies in the flavorful meatballs made with 3 kinds of meat.

Serves 8

3 (23-ounce) cans good-quality
    tomato sauce
1 (5.5-ounce) can tomato paste
1 onion, finely chopped
1 green pepper, finely chopped
1 clove garlic, minced
2 tablespoons Italian seasoning
$^1/_2$ teaspoon pepper

$^1/_2$ teaspoon salt
$^1/_3$ pound ground beef
$^1/_3$ pound ground veal
$^1/_3$ pound ground pork
1 egg
$^1/_4$ cup Italian-style bread crumbs
$^1/_4$ cup freshly grated Parmesan
    cheese

1. Combine the tomato sauce, tomato paste, onion, green pepper, garlic, Italian seasoning, pepper, and salt in the slow cooker.
2. In a large bowl, combine the beef, veal, pork, egg, bread crumbs, and Parmesan; form into balls.
3. Transfer the meatballs to the slow cooker.
4. Cook on LOW for 8 to 10 hours, or on HIGH for 4 to 5 hours.

 Tip: Serve over spaghetti or your other favorite pasta. To make sure pasta is well coated with sauce, return drained pasta to the pot you cooked it in, add a cup or so of sauce, and mix well. Serve with additional sauce and meatballs over the top.

Cheesy Pasta and Beef Casserole

33 Minutes

*Let Hubby and the kids fend for themselves with
this easy-to-preassemble casserole.*

Serves 4
1 pound lean ground beef
1 onion, chopped
4 cups uncooked pasta
1 cup grated Cheddar cheese
1 cup grated mozzarella cheese
1 cup plus 3 tablespoons tomato sauce
3 tablespoons freshly grated Parmesan cheese

1. In a skillet, cook the ground beef and onion over medium-high heat until the meat is no longer pink.
2. Meanwhile, cook the pasta until not quite done.
3. Transfer well-drained beef and pasta to the slow cooker, and stir in the Cheddar cheese, mozzarella cheese, and 1 cup of the tomato sauce.
4. Spread the 3 tablespoons tomato sauce on top, and sprinkle with Parmesan cheese.
5. Cook on LOW for 3 to 5 hours, or on HIGH for $1^{1}/_{2}$ to $2^{1}/_{2}$ hours.

 Tip: To add visual interest, try using an assortment of pasta shapes instead of just one. Make sure the shapes you choose are approximately the same size so they'll be cooked at the same time.

Tender Tasty Meat Loaf

QuickEase

Lightly seasoned Italian bread crumbs, Parmesan cheese, and diced red peppers bring a European influence to this North American classic.

Serves 4

1½ pounds lean ground beef
½ cup Italian-style bread crumbs
½ cup freshly grated Parmesan
   cheese
1 small red pepper, diced
1 small onion, diced

2 eggs, slightly beaten
1 teaspoon dried parsley
½ teaspoon pepper
¼ teaspoon salt
¼ cup tomato sauce

1. Unless your slow cooker is oval in shape, tear off a 2-foot piece of aluminum foil, cut in half lengthwise, and fold each piece in half lengthwise twice, forming strips.
2. Crisscross the strips and place in the bottom of the slow cooker and up the sides, to be used as handles.
3. In a bowl, combine all the ingredients *except* the tomato sauce.
4. Form the mixture into a ball and place it in the slow cooker, on top of the foil strips, pressing the mixture down to fit the bottom of the slow cooker.
5. Spread the tomato sauce on top.
6. Cook on LOW for 8 to 10 hours, or on HIGH for 4 to 5 hours. Remove the meat loaf using the foil "handles."

 Tip: Omit the foil basket if you have an oval-shaped slow cooker, and simply form the meat into a loaf and place it in the slow cooker.

Tortilla Meat Loaf

QuickEase

Crushed tortilla chips and salsa lend a distinctive southwestern flare to this family favorite. Sliced leftovers make awesome next-day sandwiches.

Serves 4

1½ pounds lean ground beef
1 cup crushed tortilla chips
½ cup bread crumbs
1 cup chunky-style salsa

½ teaspoon chili powder
1 egg, slightly beaten
¼ cup tomato sauce

1. Unless your slow cooker is oval in shape, tear off a 2-foot piece of aluminum foil, cut in half lengthwise, and fold each piece in half lengthwise twice, forming strips.
2. Crisscross the strips and place them in the bottom of the slow cooker and up the sides, to be used as handles.
3. In a large bowl, combine all the ingredients *except* the tomato sauce.
4. Form the mixture into a ball, and place it on top of the foil strips in the slow cooker, pressing the mixture down to fit the bottom of the slow cooker.
5. Spread the tomato sauce on top.
6. Cook on LOW for 8 to 10 hours, or on HIGH for 4 to 5 hours. Remove the meat loaf using the foil "handles."

Tip: Omit the foil basket if you have an oval-shaped slow cooker, and simply form the meat into a loaf and place it in the slow cooker.

Oxtail Ragoût

33 Minutes

Slow cooking brings out the distinct taste and texture of oxtail.
Like most stews, this is even better the next day.

Serves 4

2 pounds oxtails	1 onion, chopped
¼ cup flour	1 celery stalk, sliced
2 tablespoons oil	½ teaspoon dried
4 potatoes,	thyme
quartered	½ teaspoon pepper
2 carrots, thickly	¼ teaspoon salt
sliced	1¼ cups beef broth
1 tomato,	
chopped	

1. In a plastic bag, shake the oxtails in the flour until well coated.
2. In a skillet, brown the oxtails in the oil over medium-high heat.
3. Transfer the oxtails to the slow cooker.
4. Add all the remaining ingredients to the slow cooker, and stir to mix.
5. Cook on LOW for 10 to 12 hours.

 Tip: If oxtail is not fall-off-the-bone tender at the end of the cooking time, let it cook a few hours extra.

Things to Do Tomorrow

Stew isn't the only thing that's better the next day. Why, there's a whole list of things that seem more palatable tomorrow.

1. The first day of a breadless diet.
2. An initial consultation at the gym.
3. Shopping for a new bathing suit.
4. Your first bikini wax of the season.
5. Facing the librarian when you have books overdue since last summer.
6. Paying the video store for movies overdue since last week.
7. Attending a work function held after work hours.
8. Attending a baby shower where guests can bring their kids.
9. Going through your children's closets and organizing all the little pieces into their appropriate boxes.
10. Going through your own closet and organizing all the little pieces that no longer fit.
11. Throwing out your most comfy bra just because it's dingy, shapeless, and one of the underwires is popping out.

French White Veal Stew

QuickEase

Show off your mastery of fine French cuisine with this show-stopping dish of tender veal in a mellow white cream sauce highlighted with button mushrooms and pearl onions.

Serves 4

1½ pounds veal, cubed
2 cups small mushrooms, whole
2 cups pearl onions, whole
1 celery stalk, diced
1 clove garlic, minced
¼ teaspoon dried thyme
¼ teaspoon white pepper
1 cup chicken broth
1 bay leaf
2 tablespoons flour
½ cup cream
1 tablespoon lemon juice

1. Combine the veal, mushrooms, pearl onions, celery, garlic, thyme, white pepper, broth, and bay leaf in the slow cooker.
2. Cook on **LOW** for 8 to 10 hours, or on **HIGH** for 4 to 5 hours.
3. Discard the bay leaf; mix together the flour and cream, stir into the slow cooker, and cook for an additional 20 minutes on **HIGH**.
4. Stir in the lemon juice, and serve.

 Tip: To peel pearl onions, drop them into boiling water for 30 seconds, remove from water, cut off roots, and the skins will slip off easily.

Veal in Cremini Mushroom Sauce

QuickEase

*Tender morsels of veal in a dark, creamy mushroom sauce that's
absolutely fabulous over pasta. This is a dish that looks
as good as it sounds, and tastes as good as it looks.*

Serves 4

1½ pounds veal, cubed

3 cups cremini mushrooms

¾ cup dry white wine

½ cup water

1 clove garlic, minced

1 tablespoon butter

½ teaspoon dried sage

½ teaspoon salt

½ teaspoon pepper

2 tablespoons flour

½ cup cream

1. Combine the veal, mushrooms, wine, water, garlic, butter, sage, salt, and pepper in the slow cooker.
2. Cook on LOW for 8 to 10 hours, or on HIGH for 4 to 5 hours.
3. Mix together the flour and cream, stir it into the slow cooker, and cook for an additional 20 minutes on HIGH.

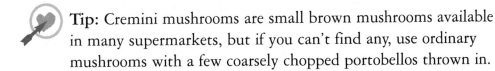 **Tip:** Cremini mushrooms are small brown mushrooms available in many supermarkets, but if you can't find any, use ordinary mushrooms with a few coarsely chopped portobellos thrown in.

Pork Chops in Fruit Smother

33 Minutes

*Golden pork chops buried beneath mounds of fruit as colorful as
a pile of autumn leaves. Destined to become a family favorite.*

Serves 4

3 strips bacon
6 pork chops, trimmed of fat
2 peaches, peeled, sliced
2 apples, peeled, sliced
1/2 cup chopped dried apricots
1/4 cup golden raisins

1/4 cup brown sugar
1 tablespoon cider vinegar
1/2 teaspoon allspice
1/4 teaspoon cinnamon
1/2 cup apple cider

1. In a large skillet, cook the bacon until just crisp, drain, and chop.
2. Brown the pork chops lightly in the bacon drippings over medium-high
   heat; then transfer to the slow cooker.
3. In a large bowl, combine the peaches, apples, apricots, raisins, brown sugar,
   cider vinegar, allspice, cinnamon, and apple cider; pour over the pork chops.
4. Sprinkle the bacon on top.
5. Cook on LOW for 4 to 5 hours, or on HIGH for 2 to 2 1/2 hours.

 Tip: Any type of pork chop will work in this recipe, so go ahead and
purchase whatever is on sale.

Apricot Pork Bake

WhamBam

Sugar and spice and everything nice, that's what pork chops with apricots and hoisin sauce are made of. Suddenly dinner is one less thing to worry about.

Serves 4

6 pork chops, trimmed of fat
$^1/_2$ cup apricot jam
3 tablespoons hoisin sauce

1. Place the pork chops in the slow cooker.
2. Mix together the apricot jam and hoisin sauce, and pour over the pork chops.
3. Cook on LOW for 5 to 6 hours, or on HIGH for $2^1/_2$ to 3 hours.

 Tip: Hoisin sauce is like a cross between soy sauce and ketchup, and is readily available in supermarkets, typically in the Asian food section.

Promises

Dear Daughter,

Part of being a mommy means making you do things you don't like. But I want you to know, there are some things I promise I will never force you to do:

1. Wear pink.
2. Wear leotards.
3. Wear the same outfit as me.
4. Eat everything on your plate.
5. Eat your words.
6. Swallow your pride.
7. Kiss butt.
8. Kiss the relatives.
9. Kiss your independence goodbye.
10. Keep up.
11. Keep out.
12. Be kept.
13. Be a cheerleader.
14. Be someone you're not.
15. Be me.

You are the love of my life, but deserve your own.

Love, Mommy

Pork Chops in Dijon Mustard Sauce

33 Minutes

Whole peppercorns add bursts of flavor to this simple dish that nicely showcases the affinity between mustard and pork.

Serves 4
1 tablespoon oil
6 pork chops, trimmed of fat
3 tablespoons flour
$1^{1}/_{2}$ cups chicken broth
2 tablespoons Dijon mustard
1 tablespoon red wine vinegar
1 teaspoon whole peppercorns

1. In a large skillet, heat the oil on medium-high and brown the pork chops lightly.
2. Transfer the pork chops to the slow cooker.
3. Sprinkle the flour into the skillet with the pork drippings and cook over medium-high heat for 1 minute, stirring constantly.
4. Add the broth, Dijon mustard, red wine vinegar, and peppercorns to the skillet, and cook over medium-high heat until the mixture thickens, stirring frequently.
5. Pour the mixture over the chops in the slow cooker.
6. Cook on LOW for 5 to 6 hours, or on HIGH for $2^{1}/_{2}$ to 3 hours.

 Tip: If you have to stack the chops in the slow cooker to make them fit, make sure each is covered with sauce.

Pork Chops and Celery in Tomato-Wine Sauce

QuickEase

Submerged in a thick tomato and red wine sauce, pork chops and celery bites are transformed into Mediterranean magic.

Serves 4

6 pork chops, trimmed of fat
3 celery stalks, cut into 1-inch lengths
2 cloves garlic, minced
1 bay leaf
1 (14-ounce) can diced tomatoes
1/2 cup dry red wine
3 tablespoons tomato paste
1 teaspoon orange zest
1/4 teaspoon dried marjoram
1/4 teaspoon salt
1/4 teaspoon pepper

1. Place the pork chops in the slow cooker, and sprinkle the celery, garlic, and bay leaf on top.
2. In a bowl, mix together the remaining ingredients and pour the mixture into the slow cooker.
3. Cook on LOW for 5 to 6 hours, or on HIGH for 2 1/2 to 3 hours.
4. Discard the bay leaf, and serve.

Tip: Zest is the colored part of a citrus rind.

On Porking Out

There are few things more dreadful than half-an-hour on a treadmill, yet few things more appealing than a firm butt. This is only one of the horrific tricks life plays on us, and every woman, at some point, must stand with her back toward a full-length mirror, her head twisted *Exorcist*-style over her shoulder, and truly assess her hindquarters. She can ignore the view and choose to believe a merciful God didn't give her eyes at the back of her head for a reason. Or, she must drag the sorry remains of what was once a thing of beauty to the gym, and run, run, run, for her life, run in an attempt to outrun time, which has such stamina that she may find herself running—even with 1 foot in the grave. Still, nice to know we have a choice.

Rosemary-Potato Pork Chops

QuickEase

*When a cold hard veggie lies down with an unyielding hunk of meat,
and together they spend the afternoon side by side beneath a blanket
of cream of potato soup, both turn out tender, inseparable, one.*

Serves 4
6 pork chops, trimmed of fat
2 teaspoons dried rosemary
2 onions, cut into rings
1 celery stalk, sliced
1 (10-ounce) can cream of potato soup
1 teaspoon Worcestershire sauce

1. Place the pork chops in the slow cooker, and sprinkle the
   rosemary, onion, and celery on top.
2. Mix together the soup and Worcestershire sauce, and pour
   over the pork chops.
3. Cook on LOW for 5 to 6 hours, or on HIGH for 2½ to
   3 hours.

 Tip: If you have a large, oval slow cooker, you may wish
to add cubed potatoes and sliced carrots to this recipe
so it becomes a 1-pot meal. Place the vegetables at the
bottom of the slow cooker, and then pile the pork chops
and other ingredients on top.

Spice-of-Life Pork Chop Bake

QuickEase

Chipotle pepper sauce adds smoke and heat to this dish, but feel free to use your favorite pepper sauce and adjust the amount according to its heat.

Serves 4

6 pork chops, trimmed of fat
1 onion, cut into rings
1 green pepper, cut into rings
1 cup tomato sauce
2 tablespoons chipotle pepper sauce
1 teaspoon dried oregano

1. Place the pork chops in the slow cooker, and cover with onion and green pepper rings.
2. Mix together the tomato sauce and chipotle pepper sauce, and pour over the pork chops.
3. Sprinkle the oregano on top.
4. Cook on LOW for 5 to 6 hours, or on HIGH for 2½ to 3 hours.

 Tip: Among the latest pepper sauces to hit the market, chipotle (pronounced chee-POHT-lay) peppers are actually smoked jalapeños.

Life's Hot New Enemy

In the past, a lot of women complained about their mothers-in-law. Today, many have a new enemy to face. She's called your husband's ex-wife, and baby, she can make your mother-in-law look like Mrs. Claus. Sure, your mother-in-law may meddle in your business, but the ex-wife and her legal team can invade your privacy and your bank account. Sure, your mother-in-law may tell you how to raise your children, but the ex-wife can tell you how to raise *hers* every other weekend, holidays, and school break. Sure, your mother-in-law may think her son's the greatest, but the ex-wife can have such a love/hate thing going for your husband, you won't know if she wants him back, or dead. And so what if your mother-in-law flashes around old pictures of your hubby naked in the tub? So too may the ex-wife!

Cider-and-Honey-Glazed Pork Roast

33 Minutes

A fabulous feast as fitting as football in the fall.

Serves 6
3-pound pork shoulder roast, boneless
1/4 cup cider
1/4 cup honey
1/4 cup fancy molasses
1 tablespoon Dijon mustard
1 tablespoon hoisin sauce

1. Place the roast in the slow cooker, and pour the cider over the top.
2. Cook on LOW for 6 to 8 hours, or on HIGH for 3 to 4 hours.
3. Preheat oven to 325°. In a bowl, mix together the remaining ingredients.
4. Transfer the roast to roasting pan, and pour the honey mixture over the top.
5. Cook uncovered in the oven for 45 minutes.

Tip: While not as lean as other cuts of pork, shoulder roast is ideal for this recipe because it will remain moist through the slow-cooking and baking processes. For easy cleanup, line the bottom of the roasting pan with foil.

At What Price Glory?

I want to be one of those moms who look great even at a kid's Saturday morning football game. The type who can climb the bleachers in heels, and not freeze wearing a T-shirt and vest. A woman whose just-got-out-of-bed hairstyle doesn't look like she just got out of bed. And whose eyes are lined with a charcoal pencil instead of woke-up-at-the-crack-of-dawn crust. I want to be one of those women who wouldn't be caught dead wearing her fat-day jeans in public, or a sweatshirt if she's over size 3. Who knows how to choose sunglasses that make her look like a movie star, not a bug. And whose handbag matches her belt, which matches her boots, which match the interior of her car. *Hmm.* I wonder how early I'd have to get up. Okay, I'm doing it . . . starting next year.

Pork Roast in Red Pepper Jelly Sauce

QuickEase

*Impress your guests with succulent pork roast and potatoes
bathed in a divine red pepper jelly sauce.*

Serves 6

5 potatoes, cubed

3-pound pork loin roast,
    boneless

¹/₂ cup red pepper jelly

1 tablespoon soy sauce

1 teaspoon ground ginger

¹/₂ teaspoon Dijon
    mustard

¹/₄ teaspoon salt

¹/₄ teaspoon pepper

1 onion, cut into rings

1 red pepper, slivered

1. Place the potatoes in the slow cooker, and set the pork roast
   on top.
2. In a bowl, combine the red pepper jelly, soy sauce, ginger,
   Dijon mustard, salt, and pepper; pour over the pork roast.
3. Sprinkle the onion rings and red pepper slivers on top of the
   pork roast.
4. Cook on LOW for 6 to 8 hours, or on HIGH for 3 to 4 hours.

 Tip: If you like sweet potatoes, use them instead, or throw
in a few along with regular potatoes.

BBQ Pork Roast

QuickEase

Everyone from Grandma to the kids will enjoy tender, juicy slices of pork roast with plenty of flavorful red gravy on the side.

Serves 6

3-pound pork shoulder roast, boneless

1 onion, chopped

2 cloves garlic, minced

1 (10-ounce) can condensed tomato soup

2 tablespoons Worcestershire sauce

2 tablespoons brown sugar

1 teaspoon dry mustard

1/4 teaspoon salt

2 tablespoons flour

1/4 cup water

1. Place the pork roast in the slow cooker, and sprinkle with the onions and garlic.
2. In a bowl, mix together the soup, Worcestershire sauce, brown sugar, dry mustard, and salt; pour over the roast.
3. Cook on LOW for 6 to 8 hours, or on HIGH for 3 to 4 hours.
4. Remove the roast and keep warm.
5. Mix together the flour and water, whisk into the slow cooker, and cook for an additional 20 minutes on HIGH.

 Tip: If there's a lot of fat in the juices, tilt the slow cooker and skim off some of the fat prior to adding the flour mixture.

Honey-Plum Country Ribs

33 Minutes

*Even finicky city slickers will love these country-style
ribs basted in a lick-your-lips plum sauce
sweetened with great gobs of honey.*

Serves 4

3 pounds country-style pork ribs, cut into single sections
1/4 teaspoon pepper
1/2 cup plum sauce
1/2 cup honey
2 teaspoons soy sauce

1. Broil ribs for 20 minutes, turning once.
2. Transfer to slow cooker, and sprinkle with pepper.
3. In a bowl, mix together the plum sauce, honey, and soy
   sauce, and pour over ribs.
4. Cook on **LOW** for 6 to 8 hours, or on **HIGH** for 3 to
   4 hours.

 Tip: If your slow cooker isn't large enough to lay ribs
in a single layer, make sure each rib is covered in sauce,
and stir once at halftime if you can.

Chili-Spiced Country Ribs

33 Minutes

*Thick slabs of pork treated to a spicy rub, then
slow cooked in a barbecue-salsa sauce.*

Serves 4
3 teaspoons chili powder
1 teaspoon ground cumin
1/2 teaspoon pepper
1/4 teaspoon cayenne
3 pounds country-style pork ribs, cut into single sections
1 cup bottled barbecue sauce
1/2 cup bottled chunky salsa

1. In a small bowl, combine the chili powder, cumin, pepper, and cayenne, and sprinkle over both sides of each rib.
2. Broil the ribs for 20 minutes, turning once.
3. Transfer ribs to slow cooker.
4. In a bowl, mix together the barbecue sauce and salsa, and pour over the ribs.
5. Cook on LOW for 6 to 8 hours, or on HIGH for 3 to 4 hours.

 Tip: For maximum flavor, use a good-quality barbecue sauce in this recipe. Choose mild, medium, or hot salsa depending on your taste, but keep in mind, the spices called for already pack a lot of punch!

Lion's Head Pork Balls

QuickEase

*A Chinese classic. Pork balls (which supposedly resemble lions' heads)
and cabbage (their manes!) cuddle up in a tasty dark broth.*

Serves 4
2 cups shredded cabbage
1 1/2 pounds ground pork
1 tablespoon sherry
2 teaspoons soy sauce
1/2 teaspoon ground ginger
1/2 teaspoon pepper
2 cups chicken broth

1. Place the cabbage in the slow cooker, and create a well in the middle so the cabbage resembles a nest.
2. In a bowl, mix together the pork, sherry, soy sauce, ginger, and pepper, and form into 8 balls.
3. Transfer the balls to the "nest" in the slow cooker.
4. Carefully pour the broth over the cabbage, but not directly on top of the pork balls.
5. Cook on LOW for 6 to 8 hours.

 Tip: Serve cabbage and pork balls with a bit of broth in wide, shallow soup bowls.

Hear Me Roar

Reasons it's great to be a woman:

1. When events occur once a year for your entire lifetime, you can retain the date in your head.
2. When you've got 2 or more things to do at once, you call it life, not multitasking.
3. When your underwear have more holes than your colander, you know it's time to throw them out.
4. When people drop by for a friendly visit, you accept you may have to speak.
5. When someone asks if you have gas, you know they're referring to your car.
6. When your spouse is going out for the afternoon, he wouldn't dare write a list of things for you to do.
7. When you behave badly you have a once-a-month excuse, and nobody keeps track of when it is.
8. When you wake up in the morning, the only thing sticking up is your hair.

Hot-and-Sour Pork

QuickEase

Bits of hot chili pepper, sweet pineapple, tender pork, and crunchy baby corn add up to a symphony of flavor, texture, and color in this gorgeous Asian delight.

Serves 4

1 pound pork, cubed	1 (14-ounce) can pineapple
1 green pepper, chopped	chunks, undrained
1 red chili pepper, diced	1/2 cup chicken broth
1 tablespoon rice vinegar	2 tablespoons cornstarch
1 tablespoon soy sauce	2 tablespoons water
1 teaspoon ground ginger	1 (14-ounce) can baby corn,
1 teaspoon Chinese 5-spice	drained

1. Combine the pork, pepper, chili pepper, rice vinegar, soy sauce, ginger, Chinese 5-spice, pineapple with juice, and broth in the slow cooker.
2. Cook on LOW for 5 to 6 hours, or on HIGH for 2 1/2 to 3 hours.
3. Mix together the cornstarch and water, and stir into the slow cooker.
4. Add the corn to the slow cooker, and cook for an additional 20 minutes on HIGH.

 Tip: Lovely served with your favorite type of rice or rice noodles.

Sweet-and-Sour Pork

QuickEase

*Chunks of pineapple, green pepper, and pork mingle in a classic
sweet-and-sour sauce. You'll never order take-out again.*

Serves 4

1 1/2 pounds pork, cubed

1 green pepper, chopped

1 onion, chopped

1 (14-ounce) can pineapple
  chunks, with juice

1/2 cup brown sugar

1/4 cup cider vinegar

1/4 cup orange juice

2 teaspoons soy sauce

2 tablespoons cornstarch

2 tablespoons water

1. Place the pork, pepper, and onion in the slow cooker.
2. Drain the pineapple, reserving chunks for later.
3. In a bowl, combine the pineapple juice, brown sugar, cider
   vinegar, orange juice, and soy sauce; stir into slow cooker.
4. Cook on LOW for 5 to 6 hours, or on HIGH for 2 1/2 to 3 hours.
5. Mix together the cornstarch and water, and stir into the slow
   cooker.
6. Stir in the pineapple chunks, and cook for an additional 20
   minutes on HIGH.

 Tip: If you have them on hand, throw in chopped carrots and
red peppers to add color and crunch.

Brown Sugar Cottage Roll

33 Minutes

A nice change from ham, here, cured pork is slow cooked for hours, and then baked in a brown sugar glaze. Pour extra glaze over everything on your plate.

Serves 4

2-pound cottage roll	1 bay leaf
5 whole cloves	Water to cover
5 peppercorns	1 cup brown sugar

1. Rinse the cottage roll.
2. Place all the ingredients *except* the brown sugar in the slow cooker.
3. Cook on LOW for 6 to 8 hours, or on HIGH for 3 to 4 hours.
4. Preheat oven to 325°. Reserve 1/4 cup of hot liquid from the slow cooker, transfer the cottage roll to a baking dish, and cut off the string securing the cottage roll.
5. Mix the brown sugar with the hot liquid, and pour over the cottage roll.
6. Bake uncovered for 1 1/2 hours; serve with glaze on the side.

 Tip: If a cottage roll is unavailable, substitute smoked ham, use only 1/2 cup of water, and reduce cooking time to 4 hours on LOW.

Oh, the Depressing Things We Buy . . .

1. Home gym equipment—Feel guilty every time you dust it.
2. Granny panties—What the hell, no one important is gonna see them.
3. Nursing pads—Not even Earth Mothers like these babies.
4. Wrinkle-removal cream—Hey, maybe it works on linen.
5. Cellulite-removal cream—Just buy the stuff and stop blubbering.
6. Hair removal kits—What could be worse than making hot wax and pouring it all over your skin?
7. Facial-hair removal kits—Okay, that's worse.
8. Diet food—Less yum, less bum.
9. Those stick-on things that are supposed to hold your boobs up—Ya had to buy a halter top, didn't ya?
10. The next-size-up jeans—Repeat after me: The designers are making them smaller; the designers are making them smaller . . .

Ham with Island Fruit

QuickEase

Ham is treated to a tropical paradise of pineapple, papaya, and mango bathed in a sweet and syrupy ginger sauce.

Serves 6
2 cups mixture of dried pineapple, papaya, and mango
Hot water to cover
3-pound smoked ham
1 cup brown sugar
2 pieces crystallized ginger, chopped
$1/4$ teaspoon cinnamon

1. Let dried fruit soak in enough hot water to cover for 10 minutes.
2. Meanwhile, using a sharp knife, make crisscross slits on the outer surface of the ham.
3. Drain fruit, reserving juice.
4. Transfer the fruit and ham to the slow cooker.
5. In a bowl, mix together $1/2$ cup of the reserved juice, the brown sugar, ginger, and cinnamon, and pour over fruit and ham.
6. Cook on LOW for 6 to 8 hours, or on HIGH for 3 to 4 hours.

 Tip: Experiment with different types of dried fruit, including traditional standbys such as apples and peaches.

Sweet Potato and Ham Jam

WhamBam

A Hawaiian-inspired dish that marries cubes of sweet potatoes and ham with tropical pineapple jam. Serve wearing a grass skirt.

Serves 4

4 sweet potatoes, cubed
1 large cooked ham steak, cubed
1½ cups pineapple jam

1. Spray the slow cooker with nonstick spray.
2. Combine all the ingredients in the slow cooker.
3. Cook on LOW for 5 to 7 hours.

Tip: Experiment with the variety of tropical jams available these days, such as mango and papaya.

Pass the Jam

Everybody has one: a girlfriend who seems to call only when she's in a jam—which, in itself, you could probably live with, if only she understood the meaning of *jam*. For instance, if she's stuck in traffic and her husband's having heart surgery and little Joey needs to be picked up after school, well, hell, that's a jam. But if she's stuck in traffic, her fully recovered husband is golfing, and dear Joey needs a ride to a birthday party, well, that's more like a pickle. And if she's stuck in line waiting to do lunch on some outdoor patio, her husband's off boozing with his buddies, and Joey-the-brat wants to go the video store, well, that's a piece of cake. And anyone who would drop what they're doing and run to her rescue every time she calls, well—I guess that makes me a nut.

Spicy Sausage, Onion, and Pepper Layer

33 Minutes

*Sausage slices nestled between layers of onions and peppers and smothered
in a robust tomato sauce create an awesome dish that begs to
be washed down with red wine.*

Serves 4

2 pounds hot Italian sausage	4 bay leaves	¹/₂ cup dry red wine
1 large onion, sliced	1 teaspoon dried basil	2 tablespoons chopped fresh parsley
1 green pepper, chopped	1 (28-ounce) can diced tomatoes, drained, juice reserved	1 tablespoon dried oregano
1 red pepper, chopped	1 (5.5-ounce) can tomato paste	¹/₂ teaspoon salt
4 cloves garlic, minced		¹/₄ teaspoon pepper

1. Poke a few holes in the sausages; bake in a 375° oven for 20 minutes, drain off the fat, and slice the sausages.
2. Layer half the onion on the bottom of the slow cooker, then half the green pepper, half the red pepper, and all the sliced sausages.
3. Add layers of the remaining onion and peppers, and sprinkle garlic, bay leaves, basil, and tomatoes on top.
4. In a bowl, mix the reserved tomato juice with the tomato paste and red wine, and pour over the top.
5. Cook on LOW for 6 to 8 hours, or on HIGH for 3 to 4 hours.
6. Sprinkle the parsley, oregano, salt, and pepper over the top, and cook for an additional 1 hour on LOW.

 Tip: This dish is fabulous served with pasta and bread to sop up the sauce.

Poodle Noodles and Wienee Dogz

33 Minutes

Spiral pasta and lengths of wieners in a mild creamy sauce are sure to be gobbled up by the kids. It's mac and cheese at its finest.

Serves 4

3 cups uncooked spiral-shaped pasta
2 tablespoons butter
2 tablespoons flour
1/2 teaspoon salt
1/4 teaspoon pepper
1 1/2 cups milk
1/4 teaspoon dry mustard
2 1/2 cups grated Cheddar cheese
4 wieners, cut into 1-inch lengths

1. Cook the pasta until not quite done, drain, and transfer to the slow cooker.
2. Meanwhile, in a saucepan, melt the butter over medium heat, and whisk in the flour, salt, and pepper.
3. Whisk in the milk and dry mustard, and bring to a boil, continuing to whisk until the mixture thickens.
4. Stir in 2 cups of the cheese and the wieners.
5. Transfer the mixture to the slow cooker, combine with the pasta, and sprinkle the remaining cheese over the top.
6. Cook on LOW for 3 to 4 hours.

 Tip: Experiment with different cheeses such as Monterey jack and mozzarella.

White Beans and Kielbasa

QuickEase

*A distant cousin of pork and beans, this feast of white
legumes and spicy sausage is a garlic lover's delight.
True garlic-heads may throw in an extra clove.*

Serves 4

1/2 pound kielbasa, skin removed, quartered and sliced
2 (19-ounce) cans white kidney beans, rinsed and drained
1 onion, whole
1 garlic clove, crushed
2 tablespoons sugar
1 cup water

1. Combine all the ingredients in the slow cooker.
2. Cook on **LOW** for 3 to 4 hours.
3. Discard the onion and garlic, and serve.

 Tip: To round off the meal, serve with salad and crusty
bread. The kielbasa called for in this recipe is the cooked,
smoked variety available in the deli section of the
supermarket.

Lamb Chops in Vegetable Mustard Medley

QuickEase

A slight twist on a fabulous French casserole. Here, lamb chops are buried beneath a medley of vegetables, mellowing to melt-in-your-mouth perfection.

Serves 4

6 lamb shoulder chops
2 potatoes, diced
2 carrots, sliced
1 celery stalk, sliced
1 onion, chopped
1 parsnip, sliced
1 clove garlic, minced

1 (19-ounce) can diced tomatoes
1/2 cup chicken broth
1 1/2 teaspoons prepared mustard
1 teaspoon dried mint
1 teaspoon dried parsley
1/4 teaspoon dried thyme

1. Place the lamb chops in the slow cooker, and place the potatoes, carrots, celery, onion, parsnip, and garlic on top.
2. In a bowl, combine the tomatoes, broth, mustard, mint, parsley, and thyme; pour the mixture into the slow cooker over the lamb chops and vegetables.
3. Cook on LOW for 6 to 8 hours, or on HIGH for 3 to 4 hours.

 Tip: The taste of lamb is subdued in this dish, so even those who snub lamb are encouraged to give it a try.

Lamb Chops in White Wine Sauce

WhamBam

It tastes as though you've been in the kitchen all day. Does anyone really have to know that you slapped together this elegant dish in minutes?

Serves 4

2 onions, sliced

6 lamb shoulder chops

1 (14-ounce) can white wine and
   cream sauce

1. Place the onions in the slow cooker, and place the lamb chops on top.
2. Pour the white wine and cream sauce over the top.
3. Cook on **LOW** for 6 to 8 hours, or on **HIGH** for 3 to 4 hours.

Tip: Not to worry, juices from the lamb greatly enhance the flavor of canned sauce.

A B-a-a-a-d Experience

One morning, I was all set to make dinner but when I opened the lamb, it was off. I checked the expiration date, and sure enough, it said 2 days from now. Super mad, I grabbed the meat and rushed to the supermarket.

"Take a whiff of this!" I ordered the customer service girl, flinging the package on the counter. "This lamb is bad! All I wanted to do is feed my family, and now my whole morning is shot!"

My mild hysteria drew a small crowd. *So what?* I thought. Let 'em hear. After all, this is a *food safety* issue.

"It's a good thing I'm on the ball," I continued, "or I could have poisoned my loved ones. Look at the sticker. It says the lamb is good till Monday!"

The girl glanced at the package briefly.

"But that's not our sticker, ma'am," she cooed. "You bought this at our competitor's."

I apologized, never having felt so . . . *sheepish.*

Lamb Chops in Tomato-Oregano Sauce

QuickEase

*A perfect example of how a few readily available
ingredients can turn economical cuts of lamb
into a tasty Mediterranean meal.*

Serves 4

6 lamb shoulder chops
2 onions, thinly sliced into rings
2 cloves garlic, minced
1 (23-ounce) can tomato sauce
2 teaspoons dried oregano
$1/2$ teaspoon dried mint
$1/2$ teaspoon salt
$1/4$ teaspoon pepper

1. Place the lamb chops in the slow cooker, and place the onion rings and garlic on top.
2. In a bowl, mix together the remaining ingredients, and pour the mixture over the lamb chops.
3. Cook on LOW for 6 to 8 hours, or on HIGH for 3 to 4 hours.

 Tip: All cuts of lamb are quite tender, but chops from the rib and loin sections are even more so, and thus, very expensive. Save money by purchasing shoulder chops, which will turn out fabulously tender in your slow cooker.

Lamb Morocco

QuickEase

A spicy lamb concoction that unites tomatoes with turmeric and a hit of red pepper flakes to spice it up. Raisins sweeten the deal.

Serves 4

1 1/2 pounds lamb stew meat
1 onion, chopped
1 celery stalk, sliced
1 clove garlic, minced
1 (19-ounce) can diced tomatoes
1/3 cup chicken broth
1/3 cup raisins
2 tablespoons tomato paste
1/4 teaspoon turmeric
1/4 teaspoon red pepper flakes
1/4 teaspoon pepper

1. Combine all the ingredients in the slow cooker.
2. Cook on **LOW** for 8 to 10 hours, or on **HIGH** for 4 to 5 hours.

 Tip: Lamb Morocco is lovely over rice, or with couscous on the side.

Cell Hell

Warning: Bringing your cell phone on a night out with the girls can be hazardous. *Rrriiinnnggg.* Hello? Hi, Hon. No, we lost the game, so we're drowning our sorrows in wine. Not long, maybe another 45 minutes. Ish. Pardon? Oh, just read 'em a story and put 'em to bed. Okay. Love ya, bye. *Rrriiinnnggg.* Hello? I don't know, Three Little Pigs or Bears or whatever. No, we haven't even ordered yet. Bye. *Rrriiinnnggg.* Yeah? Look under her bed, or just give her another stuffed animal and say Pooshka came to volleyball with me. Fine. *Rrriiin–* WHAT? Aw geez no, don't put her—oh, hi Sweetie-Pie. No, Mommy's still playing. I can't leave, Honey-Bunny, the team needs me. Tell Daddy to tuck you in and I'll be home soon. Bye-bye. *Rrrr–* WHAT THE HELL DO YOU WANT NOW? Sweetie? Sorry, Mommy thought you were someone else. When did you learn to dial Mommy's cell? Daddy taught you? That's so nice . . .

Irish Stew

QuickEase

*If your husband is a lamb-loving, meat-and-potatoes kind of guy,
he'll go crazy over this Irish classic.*

Serves 4

1 1/2 pounds lamb stew meat
5 potatoes, cubed
3 carrots, thickly sliced
2 onions, quartered
1/2 teaspoon pepper
1/4 teaspoon dried thyme
1/4 teaspoon dried marjoram
2 cups beef broth
3 tablespoons flour
1/4 cup water

1. Combine all the ingredients *except* the flour and water in the slow cooker.
2. Cook on LOW for 8 to 10 hours, or on HIGH for 4 to 5 hours.
3. Mix together the flour and water, stir it into the slow cooker, and cook for an additional 20 minutes on HIGH.

 Tip: Traditional Irish Stew features more potatoes than meat, so throw in extra potatoes, if you wish.

Something to Stew About

Every now and then my husband goes on a rampage about bills.

"Do you know how much we spend on electricity?" he asks my daughter, who is working on her computer, which is next to her lava lamp, which is next to her stereo system.

"Have you seen these phone bills?" he asks my son, who is engaged in a 3-way phone call while his cell phone charges and he chats online.

"Look at our water bills!" Hubby wails, finding me soaking in the tub. Nearby, the washing machine washes, the pool over-fills, and the sprinkler waters the driveway.

"That's it!' he declares. "I'm gonna pull the plug on it all!"

An idle threat, but I move my heel closer to the drain just in case.

Lamb in Ginger-Pear Wine Sauce with Lima Beans

33 Minutes

Fresh pears, sautéed in ginger, white wine, and a hint of mint, lighten and invigorate tender cubes of lamb.

Serves 4

1½ pounds lamb stew meat	1 teaspoon ground ginger
1 tablespoon oil	½ teaspoon dried mint
4 pears, peeled, cubed	¼ teaspoon salt
1 cup frozen lima beans	½ cup dry white wine

1. In a large skillet, brown the lamb lightly in oil over medium-high heat.
2. Using a slotted spoon, transfer the lamb to the slow cooker.
3. Add the pears, lima beans, ginger, mint, and salt to the skillet and cook over medium heat for 4 minutes, stirring frequently.
4. Add the wine and bring the mixture to a boil; reduce heat, and let cook for 3 minutes.
5. Transfer the mixture to the slow cooker.
6. Cook on LOW for 6 to 8 hours, or on HIGH for 3 to 4 hours.

Tip: If lima beans are unavailable, use frozen peas or string beans instead.

Curried Lamb with Prunes and Apricots

QuickEase

In this exotic dish, bites of sweet fruit dance in a spicy lamb and potato medley providing mouthful after mouthful of pleasure.

Serves 4

1 1/2 pounds lamb stew meat
3 potatoes, cubed
1 onion, chopped
1/2 cup chopped prunes
1/2 cup chopped dried apricots
2 teaspoons curry powder
1/8 teaspoon cayenne
1/2 cup chicken broth

1. Combine all the ingredients in the slow cooker.
2. Cook on LOW for 8 to 10 hours, or on HIGH for 4 to 5 hours.

 Tip: Not all curry powder brands are created equal, so purchase curry powder in small quantities until you find your favorite.

A Hairy Experience

Omigod! I just met the hairstylist from hell! First, I show her a picture of this exotic woman I want to look like, and she makes a joke about being a hairdresser, not a plastic surgeon. When I don't laugh, she says I might look cool with purple streaks. So, I say, "Only hairdressers can wear that weirdo look." So, she starts giving me a hairstyle I'll never be able to re-create at home. So, I say, "Give me something simple—if I were good with a curling iron, I wouldn't be here, would I?" Then, I launch into my highly interesting life story, and rather than marvel at my accomplishments, she just fiddles with my hair and tells me I've got a big head! Finally, she gives me an outrageous bill. I remind her she's a hairdresser, not a plastic surgeon—and she throws me out! The *nerve*.

Chicken in Tomato-Basil Sauce

33 Minutes

*Cloaked in a sumptuous tomato-basil sauce, golden pieces of
chicken await a date with your favorite pasta.*

Serves 4

3 pounds chicken pieces (mixture
    of dark and white meat)
1 tablespoon olive oil
1 onion, chopped

2 cloves garlic, minced
1 (28-ounce) can plum tomatoes
3 tablespoons tomato paste
2 teaspoons dried basil

1. To reduce the fat, remove the skin from the dark meat.
2. In a large skillet, brown the chicken pieces lightly in oil over
   medium-high heat.
3. Using a slotted spoon, transfer the chicken to the slow cooker.
4. Add the onion and garlic to the skillet and cook over medium-high
   heat for 3 minutes.
5. Stir in the tomatoes, tomato paste, and basil, and bring to a boil.
6. Transfer the mixture to the slow cooker.
7. Cook on LOW for 6 to 8 hours, or on HIGH for 3 to 4 hours.

Tip: For a pretty presentation, sprinkle the rims of the serving plates
with freshly chopped parsley, place the chicken and pasta in the
center, and sprinkle more parsley over the top.

Lemon-Garlic Chicken on a Vegetable Bed

QuickEase

*Golden chicken pieces infused with lemon and garlic,
slow cooked to tender perfection, and served on a
bed of baby carrots and caramelized onions.*

Serves 4

4 pounds chicken pieces (mixture
    of dark and white meat)

2 cups baby carrots

3 onions, quartered

2 tablespoons butter

1/2 cup chicken broth

2 tablespoons oil

2 tablespoons lemon juice

3 cloves garlic, chopped

1 tablespoon dried oregano

2 teaspoons dried parsley

1/4 teaspoon white pepper

1. To reduce the fat, remove the skin from the dark meat.
2. Combine the carrots and onions in the slow cooker, dollop with butter, and pour broth over the top.
3. Mix together the oil and lemon juice, brush the chicken with the mixture, and place in the slow cooker on top of the vegetables.
4. Sprinkle the garlic, oregano, parsley, and white pepper over the top.
5. Cook on LOW for 6 to 8 hours, or on HIGH for 3 to 4 hours.

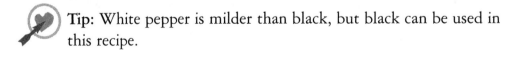 **Tip:** White pepper is milder than black, but black can be used in this recipe.

Cranberry Chicken Quarters

WhamBam

Tangy cranberry chicken pieces jazzed up with honey and garlic. You'll be tempted to lift the lid and sample . . . but do wait until it's done.

Serves 4

4 chicken quarters, skin removed
1 (14-ounce) can whole berry
    cranberry sauce
$1/2$ cup honey-garlic sauce

1. Place the chicken quarters in the slow cooker.
2. In a bowl, mix together the cranberry sauce and honey-garlic sauce, and pour over the chicken.
3. Cook on LOW for 6 to 8 hours, or on HIGH for 3 to 4 hours.

 Tip: To remove the skin from the chicken quarters, slip your fingers beneath the skin at the thigh, and pull toward the drumstick end.

Sample This

Dear Fellow Shopper,

It's about your behavior at food sampling booths. I see you hovering around pretending to be interested in nearby products but just waiting to pounce on the poor Sample Lady the second her microwave beeps. And then saying you need 3 chicken portions—1 for your husband, 1 for your kid, blah, blah, blah, when everybody knows you're going to sneak into the next aisle and hork 'em all. And funny how you seem to shop only during lunch and dinner hours, *prime* sampling time. You're supposed to just happen to be there, like, oh, what a nice surprise, they're handing out free grub! And, one more thing: Stop chatting up the Sample Lady as if you're going to buy her product. The rest of us are starving to death behind you, so just quaff and take off, okay?

Regards,
Ima Testy

Caribbean Chicken

QuickEase

Although some dishes remind us of their origins, others, such as this one, transport us there. Chicken, vegetables, and spices in coconut milk capture all things Caribbean.

Serves 4

3 pounds chicken pieces (mixture of dark and white meat)
1 tablespoon oil
4 potatoes, cubed
3 tomatoes, chopped
1 onion, chopped
1 green pepper, chopped
1 clove garlic, minced

1 tablespoon brown sugar
1 teaspoon ground ginger
1 teaspoon pepper
1/4 teaspoon cayenne
1/4 teaspoon dried thyme
1/4 teaspoon salt
1/2 cup chicken broth
1 1/2 cups coconut milk

1. To reduce the fat, remove the skin from the dark meat.
2. In a skillet, brown the chicken in oil over medium-high heat.
3. Using a slotted spoon, transfer the chicken to the slow cooker, and add the potatoes and tomatoes to the slow cooker.
4. Add the onion, green pepper, garlic, brown sugar, ginger, pepper, cayenne, thyme, and salt to the skillet, and cook over medium-high heat for 3 minutes.
5. Stir the broth into the skillet, then transfer the mixture to the slow cooker.
6. Cook on LOW for 6 to 8 hours, or on HIGH for 3 to 4 hours.
7. Stir in the coconut milk, and cook for an additional 30 minutes on LOW.

 Tip: This is a relatively mild version of Caribbean chicken, so if you'd like to spice it up, double or triple the cayenne.

Ajiaco

*From South America comes this sultry dish featuring yucca and chicken
in a milky pool of onions, spices, and lime. The cayenne pepper
adds considerable heat; serve only to those who can take it.*

Serves 4

1 large yucca, peeled, chopped
1½ pounds chicken thighs, boneless, skinless
1 onion, chopped
1 cup chicken broth
1 teaspoon paprika
½ teaspoon cayenne
1½ cups milk
1 cup frozen corn kernels
Juice of 1 lime

1. Combine the yucca, chicken, onion, broth, paprika, and cayenne
   in the slow cooker.
2. Cook on LOW for 6 to 8 hours, or on HIGH for 3 to 4 hours.
3. Stir in the milk and corn, and cook for an additional 1 hour on LOW.
4. Stir in the lime juice just before serving.

Tip: If yucca, a potato-like vegetable with barklike dark
brown skin, isn't available, use potatoes instead.

Barbecue-Marmalade Chicken

WhamBam

Marmalade adds a tropical flair to this barbecue chicken classic.
Give your family the taste of summer, year-round.

Serves 4

3 pounds chicken pieces (mixture of dark
    and white meat)
½ cup barbecue sauce
½ cup marmalade

1. To reduce the fat, remove the skin from the
   dark meat.
2. Place the chicken in the slow cooker.
3. In a bowl, mix together the barbecue sauce
   and marmalade, and pour over the chicken.
4. Cook on LOW for 6 to 8 hours, or on
   HIGH for 3 to 4 hours.

 Tip: Any barbecue sauce works fine in
this recipe, but thicker types will "cling"
to the chicken pieces better.

Hubby's Friends

I want to be a woman in a beer commercial. Not a bimbo chick—too much work—but one of those slightly-older-but-still-lovely-looking women you see hanging out at the cottage, smiling as her husband cavorts with his wild and crazy friends. You never see those guys scarfing down every last bit of chicken off the barbecue, or kneading their beer bellies at the picnic table while they eat. You never see those guys banging their heads, doing back flips off the dock, or relieving themselves in the flowerbeds. You never see those guys winking at Hubby as they babble on and on about the good old days when they picked up those hot chicks hitchhiking to Detroit. No, in a beer commercial, Hubby's wild and crazy friends behave like calm, caring, courteous men—just like in real-life, right?

Chicken and 3-Cheese Chili

33 Minutes

*More mellow than traditional beef-based chili, here chicken and white beans
bask in a mildly spiced sauce made rich and creamy with shredded cheeses.*

Serves 6

1½ pounds ground chicken
1 tablespoon oil
2 cloves garlic, minced
1 onion, chopped
1 celery stalk, diced
1 red pepper, chopped
1 teaspoon ground cumin
1 teaspoon chili powder
½ teaspoon dried oregano

½ teaspoon salt
½ teaspoon white pepper
1 (28-ounce) can tomatoes
½ cup chicken broth
1 (19-ounce) can white kidney beans,
    rinsed and drained
1 (4.5-ounce) can mild green chilies
2 cups grated cheese, mixture of Monterey
    jack, Cheddar, and mozzarella

1. In a skillet, cook the chicken in oil over medium-high heat until no longer
   pink. Using a slotted spoon, transfer the chicken to the slow cooker.
2. Add the garlic, onion, celery, red pepper, cumin, chili powder, oregano, salt,
   and white pepper to the skillet; cook over medium-high heat for 4 minutes,
   stirring frequently.
3. Add the tomatoes and broth, breaking up the tomatoes with the spoon.
4. Bring the mixture to a boil, reduce heat, and let cook for 4 minutes.
5. Transfer the mixture to the slow cooker, and stir in the beans and chilies.
6. Cook on LOW for 6 to 8 hours, or on HIGH for 3 to 4 hours.
7. Stir in the cheese mixture, and cook for an additional 20 minutes on LOW.

 Tip: For convenience, buy preshredded packages of Tex-Mex cheeses.

Chicken Crock Pie

33 Minutes

Snuggled beneath a puff pastry duvet, tender bites of chicken breast, potato, carrots, and peas bake in a dreamy tarragon-enhanced gravy.

Serves 4

1½ pounds chicken breast, boneless, skinless, cut into bite-size pieces

3 potatoes, cubed

2 carrots, diced

1 onion, chopped

1 cup chicken broth

2 teaspoons dried tarragon

1 teaspoon lemon juice

½ teaspoon pepper

¼ teaspoon salt

2 tablespoons cornstarch

2 tablespoons water

1 cup frozen peas

1 frozen puff pastry sheet, thawed

1. Combine the chicken, potatoes, carrots, onion, broth, tarragon, lemon juice, pepper, and salt in the slow cooker.
2. Cook on LOW for 6 to 8 hours.
3. Mix together the cornstarch and water and stir it into the slow cooker. Add the peas, and cook for an additional 20 minutes on LOW.
4. Preheat oven to 400°. Transfer the chicken mixture to a 9-inch deep-dish pie plate, cover with puff pastry according to package directions, and bake for 20 minutes or until golden.

Tip: If you only have a wide, shallow pie plate, thaw an extra puff pastry sheet so you'll have enough to cover. Remember to thaw puff pastry overnight in the refrigerator or on the counter for a few hours.

Chicken Curry Hurry

QuickEase

The marvelous aroma of curry awaits you after a tiresome day at work.
Kick off your shoes, and tear off that darling little suit . . .
all there is to do is make some rice.

Serves 4

1½ pounds chicken breasts, boneless, skinless, cut into bite-size pieces

1 (14-ounce) can pineapple tidbits, with juice

1 envelope chicken bouillon powder

3 teaspoons curry powder

1. Place the chicken in the slow cooker.
2. Drain the pineapple juice into small bowl, reserving the tidbits.
3. Combine the bouillon powder and curry powder with the juice, and pour over the chicken.
4. Cook on LOW for 4 to 5 hours.
5. Add the pineapple tidbits, and cook for an additional 15 minutes on LOW.

Tip: Adjust curry quantity according to taste.

A Woman's Schedule

6 A.M.	Wake up. Let dog out. Make breakfast and lunches. Get everyone out of bed.
7 A.M.	Take kids to bus stop. Let dog in. Let husband out.
8 A.M.	Pluck eyebrows on way to office.
9 A.M.	Start work.
NOON	Rush to doctor's appointment. Wait.
2 P.M.	Rush back to work. Apologize for missing beginning of meeting.
5 P.M.	Apologize for missing end of meeting. Explain got to be home for kids.
6 P.M.	Apologize to sitter. Make dinner. Do breakfast dishes. Call Hubby's cell. Forgot he's golfing. Eat with kids.
7 P.M.	Drive kids to swimming lessons.
8 P.M.	Do homework with kids. Put kids to bed. Call hubby's cell. Still golfing?
9 P.M.	Do laundry, dinner dishes, telephone banking, take-home work . . .
11 P.M.	Go to bed. Sleep.
12 A.M.	Wake up. Can't breathe. Ceiling must have fallen. Realize just Hubby, and fall back to sleep.

Pineapple-Ginger Chicken

QuickEase

Chunks of sweet pineapple and tender strips of chicken linger in a citrus–soy sauce spiked with ginger and garlic. Begs for fluffy white rice.

Serves 4

1½ pounds chicken breast, boneless, skinless, cut into strips

2 green onions, thinly sliced

1 (14-ounce) can pineapple tidbits, with juice

¼ cup chicken broth

2 tablespoons soy sauce

1 tablespoon brown sugar

½ teaspoon ground ginger

¼ teaspoon garlic powder

¼ teaspoon salt

¼ teaspoon pepper

2 tablespoons cornstarch

2 tablespoons water

1. Place the chicken and green onions in the slow cooker.
2. Drain the pineapple juice into a bowl, reserving the tidbits.
3. Combine the broth, soy sauce, brown sugar, ginger, garlic powder, salt, and pepper with the juice, and pour over the chicken.
4. Cook on LOW for 4 to 6 hours, or on HIGH for 2 to 3 hours.
5. Mix together the cornstarch and water, stir it into the slow cooker, and add the pineapple tidbits; cook for an additional 20 minutes on LOW.

 Tip: If you would like to dress up this dish, add diced carrots, celery and/or red peppers.

Sun-Dried Tomato Chicken Gumbo

33 Minutes

Beware: Cayenne pepper adds danger to the dish, causing ordinary evenings to turn spicy.

Serves 8

1 (28-ounce) can diced tomatoes

3 cups chicken broth

2 tablespoons oil

1 1/2 pounds chicken thighs, boneless, skinless, cut into bite-size pieces

1/2 cup oil

1/2 cup flour

2 celery ribs, chopped

1 onion, chopped

1 green pepper, chopped

1/2 pound Polish sausage, cut into bite-size pieces

3/4 cup chopped oil-packed sun-dried tomatoes

1/2 teaspoon black pepper

1/2 teaspoon cayenne

1/2 teaspoon garlic powder

4 cups cooked rice

1. Combine the tomatoes and broth in the slow cooker.
2. In a cast-iron skillet, heat the 2 tablespoons of oil on medium-high, and brown the chicken. Using a slotted spoon, set chicken aside.
3. Make a roux by adding the 1/2 cup of oil to the skillet, and heating it on high for 3 minutes. Reduce to medium-high, gradually add the flour, and whisk constantly for 6 minutes or until roux is reddish brown.
4. Remove from heat and add celery, onion, and pepper to the roux, stirring constantly for 3 or 4 minutes.
5. Whisk roux and vegetable mixture into slow cooker, stir in the chicken and the remaining ingredients, *except* the rice, and cook on LOW for 8 to 10 hours, or HIGH for 4 to 5 hours. Serve in bowls over rice.

 Tip: If you see dark brown flecks in the roux, it's burned. Start over.

Chicken Mole

33 Minutes

A southwestern favorite that includes an unlikely ingredient: chocolate. In this version, chicken thighs are slowly cooked in a spicy dark sauce.

Serves 4

1 tablespoon oil	¹/₄ teaspoon ground cloves
1¹/₂ pound chicken thighs, boneless, skinless	2 cups tomato sauce
1 onion, chopped	2 tablespoons chipotle pepper sauce
2 cloves garlic, minced	1 ounce (1 wrapped square) unsweetened chocolate, grated
1 teaspoon chili powder	1 tablespoon ground almonds

1. In a large skillet, heat the oil on medium-high, and brown the chicken.
2. Using a slotted spoon, transfer the chicken to the slow cooker.
3. Add the onions, garlic, chili powder, and cloves to the skillet, and cook over medium-high heat for 3 minutes, stirring constantly.
4. Add the tomato sauce and chipotle pepper sauce, and bring to a boil; reduce heat and let simmer for 4 minutes.
5. Stir in the chocolate and almonds, and transfer the mixture to the slow cooker.
6. Cook on **LOW** for 5 to 6 hours, or on **HIGH** for 2¹/₂ to 3 hours.

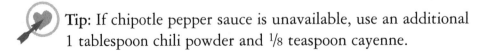

Tip: If chipotle pepper sauce is unavailable, use an additional 1 tablespoon chili powder and ¹/₈ teaspoon cayenne.

Chicken-Asparagus Dinner

QuickEase

An all-inclusive meal of tender chunks of chicken breast, cubes of potato, and whole baby carrots in a lovely ginger-asparagus-coconut sauce.

Serves 4

4 chicken breast halves, boneless, skinless, cut into bite-size pieces
3 potatoes, cubed
2 cups baby carrots
1 (10–ounce) can condensed cream of asparagus soup
3/4 cup coconut milk
1/2 teaspoon ground ginger

1. Place the chicken, potatoes, and carrots in the slow cooker.
2. In a bowl, combine the soup, coconut milk, and ginger; stir the mixture into the slow cooker.
3. Cook on LOW for 4 to 6 hours.

 Tip: Canned coconut milk is widely available in supermarkets across North America.

Can You Spot the Similarities?

A girlfriend and I got into a conversation about how to properly store and cook asparagus. (Hey, it was a slow day.) It occurred to us that this lovely vegetable was similar to something else. We're betting you can guess what it is. First, experts advise that when considering asparagus, a woman should look for spears that are firm. Apparently, those that are soft and droopy are well past their prime. Second, when storing asparagus it's okay to keep the spears on their side. But, for some complicated reason, a spear enjoys a longer, healthier existence if it's kept vertical! The same is true when cooking. For best results, a spear should be standing upright while heat is applied. And finally, because you never know where your asparagus has been, insist it is thoroughly washed before using.

Comforting Chicken Stew

QuickEase

The familiar taste of chicken blended with everyday vegetables in a soothing gravy makes for fight-free family dinners. It's every mother's dream.

Serves 4

1½ pounds chicken thighs, boneless, skinless, cut into bite-size chunks
4 potatoes, cubed
4 carrots, thickly sliced
1 onion, chopped
1½ cups chicken broth
½ teaspoon salt
½ teaspoon pepper
1 bay leaf
3 tablespoons flour
¼ cup water

1. Place all the ingredients *except* the flour and water in the slow cooker.
2. Cook on LOW for 6 to 8 hours, or on HIGH for 3 to 4 hours.
3. Remove the bay leaf. Mix together the flour and water, stir into slow cooker, and cook for an additional 20 minutes on HIGH.

Tip: Chicken breasts can be used, but cut vegetables smaller, and cook 1 or 2 hours less.

Notice of Name Change

We are gathered here today to come up with a new name for stay-at-home moms. The term is clearly unsuitable. Because it is the opposite of working moms, it implies that stay-at-home moms don't work. What is it that they do then . . . stay? And why do we call the women who chaperon school trips, drive other people's kids all over hell's half acre, and attend all the yoga classes they sign up for stay-at-home moms? Clearly, they are everywhere but. Last but not least, the term sounds too much like an order, as in: STAY AT HOME, MOM, as in, STAY, FIDO, STAY. We welcome suggestions, but ask that you avoid expressions that are patronizing, such as "domestic engineer"; confusing terms such as "work in the home" (too close to moms with home offices); and any term that even remotely suggests these women have it easy.

Chicken Stroganoff

QuickEase

Flavorful chicken thighs in a mild, soothing mushroom sauce enriched with sour cream. Bring out the egg noodles.

Serves 4

1 pound chicken thighs, boneless, skinless, cut into strips
3 cups sliced mushrooms
1 onion, chopped
1 clove garlic, minced
$1/2$ cup water
3 tablespoons tomato paste
1 teaspoon paprika
1 teaspoon dried parsley
$1/2$ teaspoon salt
$1/2$ teaspoon pepper
1 cup sour cream

1. Combine all the ingredients *except* the sour cream in the slow cooker.
2. Cook on LOW for 6 to 8 hours, or on HIGH for 3 to 4 hours.
3. Stir in the sour cream, and cook for an additional 20 minutes on LOW.

 Tip: Dieters may wish to use low-fat or light sour cream, and chicken breasts instead of thighs. If using breasts, reduce the cooking time by 1 or 2 hours.

Chicken Tarragon

WhamBam

Tender, succulent breasts of chicken surrounded in a creamy wild mushroom gravy. Tarragon elevates this absurdly easy dish to one of elegance.

Serves 4

4 chicken breast halves, with skin and
   bone
1 (10-ounce) can condensed cream of
   wild mushroom soup
2 teaspoons dried tarragon

1. Place the chicken in the slow cooker.
2. Mix together the soup and tarragon, and
   pour over the chicken.
3. Cook on LOW for 5 to 6 hours, or on
   HIGH for 2½ to 3 hours.

 Tip: Cream of wild mushroom soup is
available in many supermarkets, but
in a pinch, ordinary cream of mushroom soup will do.

BRAzarre!

Just when I thought crazy contraptions such as girdles were a thing
of the past, along comes a whole
new breed of bizarre bras! The
other day, a saleslady tried to sell
me one that moved with the click
of a button. Why would I want to?
They're not paintings I'm gonna
hang on the wall! And what's with
liquid bras? I haven't carted
around water balloons since
grade school! Worse are the bras
filled with air. What if it gets a flat?
Doesn't that mean I'll be right
back where I started?

Chicken Breasts Parmesan

Fast, easy, elegant. Dinners don't get much better than this, especially when it's something the kids will enjoy.

Serves 4
Chicken broth
4 chicken breast halves, with skin and bone
1/4 cup bottled oil-based Caesar salad dressing
2 teaspoons Italian seasoning
1/4 cup grated Parmesan cheese

1. Pour enough broth into the slow cooker to cover the bottom, 1/4-inch deep.
2. Brush the chicken breasts generously with salad dressing, and then sprinkle with Italian seasoning and Parmesan cheese.
3. Transfer the breasts to the slow cooker.
4. Cook on LOW for 5 to 6 hours.

 Tip: A few words about Parmesan cheese: The stuff that comes in graters has a mild taste, which is why it's popular with children. If purchased in chunks, the flavor ranges from mild to strong, so shop around until you find your favorite. Or, try Romano cheese, which is similar to Parmesan but a tad stronger.

Chicken with Grapefruit Splash

WhamBam

Honeyed chicken breasts are treated to a splash of citrus sunshine in this cheerful dish that goes beautifully with mixed greens for a light, easy dinner.

Serves 4
4 chicken breast halves, with skin and bone
Juice of 1 grapefruit
1/2 cup honey

1. Place the chicken in the slow cooker.
2. In a small bowl, mix together the grapefruit juice and honey, and pour over the chicken.
3. Cook on LOW for 5 to 6 hours.

Tip: Add some zip to this dish by stirring 1/2 teaspoon of ground ginger into the grapefruit juice and honey mixture. And if you have any leftover chicken breasts, wrap tightly and refrigerate. The next day, debone chicken and slice into strips; then add it to a tossed salad for a fabulous lunch!

Roasted Chicken with Hot Italian Sausage Stuffing

33 Minutes

A fabulous dinner of juicy chicken, moist stuffing, and homemade gravy.

Serves 6

2 hot Italian sausages
1 tablespoon oil
4- to 5-pound chicken, whole
3 cups bread crumbs
1/4 cup chicken broth
1 onion, diced

1 celery stalk, diced
1 tablespoon dried sage
1 teaspoon butter, melted
2 tablespoons flour
3 tablespoons water

1. Remove the sausage from casings. In a large skillet, cook the sausage in oil over medium-high heat until no longer pink.
2. Using a slotted spoon, transfer the sausage to large bowl.
3. Add the chicken to the skillet and lightly brown in sausage drippings over medium-high heat, and then transfer to work surface.
4. Add the bread crumbs, broth, onion, celery, sage, and butter to the sausage; stuff the mixture into the chicken's cavity, and truss the chicken.
5. Place a rack or trivet in the slow cooker, and put the chicken on top.
6. Cook on LOW for 8 to 10 hours, or on HIGH for 4 to 5 hours.
7. Remove the chicken and rack. Mix together the flour and water, stir into slow cooker, and cook for an additional 20 minutes on HIGH.

Tip: To brown a whole chicken, use 2 large spoons to maneuver it around. Do not use a fork, as precious juices will escape.

Funky Chicken Whole

QuickEase

Lime and garlic flavor the chicken from the inside out;
a Thai-inspired baste flavors from the outside in.

Serves 4

1 lime, halved
2 tablespoons soy sauce
1 teaspoon brown sugar
$1/4$ teaspoon ground coriander
$1/4$ teaspoon cayenne
3- to 4-pound chicken, whole
1 clove garlic

1. In a bowl, squeeze the juice from half of the lime, and stir in the soy sauce, brown sugar, coriander, and cayenne.
2. Rub the mixture into the skin of the entire chicken.
3. Place the other half of lime and the garlic clove in the chicken's cavity, truss the chicken, and place it in the slow cooker.
4. Cook on LOW for 8 to 10 hours, or on HIGH for 4 to 5 hours.

 Tip: Whatever you place in a chicken's cavity ends up flavoring the chicken, so try different herbs with half of a lemon.

Sign on Supermarket Entrance Door

To Our Valued Customers . . .

1. Our Express Lane is restricted to 10 items. No, 5 bags of potato chips, all the same brand, do not equal 1. And no, 13 items cannot be rounded down to 10.

2. Once the cashier has begun processing your order, it is rude to leave the line. To avoid forgetting items, we encourage the use of shopping lists. To avoid forgetting shopping lists, we encourage the use of pockets.

3. Our carts do not fly. Therefore, if you block an aisle, other shoppers will have no peaceful way of getting around you.

4. Our carts do not have remote controls. Therefore, abandoning yours in the parking lot is like letting loose a missile on wheels. Warning: Shop nicely. Cart Attacks are on the rise.

Poached Chicken Velouté

33 Minutes

*Velouté is the French word for "velvety," a perfect way to describe
the sauce you'll pour over slices of tender chicken.*

Serves 4

3- to 4-pound chicken, whole
1 carrot, roughly chopped
1 celery stalk, roughly chopped
1 onion, quartered
1 bay leaf
1/2 teaspoon salt

1/2 teaspoon pepper
Water to cover
5 tablespoons butter
5 tablespoons flour
1/4 teaspoon salt

1. Combine the chicken, carrot, celery, onion, bay leaf, 1/2 teaspoon salt, and pepper in the slow cooker.
2. Pour in enough water to cover the chicken.
3. Cook on **LOW** for 8 to 10 hours, or on **HIGH** for 4 to 5 hours.
4. Remove the chicken, and reserve 4 cups of hot liquid.
5. Meanwhile, in a medium-sized saucepan, melt the butter over medium heat, and whisk in the flour, stirring until smooth; cook for 2 or 3 minutes over medium heat until the mixture is lightly browned.
6. Whisk in the reserved hot liquid and the 1/4 teaspoon salt and bring the mixture to a boil; reduce heat and simmer, uncovered, for 25 minutes.
7. Remove the meat from the chicken carcass, and slice.
8. Transfer the velouté sauce to a gravy boat, and serve with sliced chicken.

 Tip: Any extra hot liquid from the slow cooker can be used as chicken broth, strengthened, if necessary, with bouillon powder or cubes.

Roasted Chicken with Lemon and Rosemary

QuickEase

A plump, moist chicken infused with the delightful trilogy of lemon, garlic, and rosemary. Leftovers are lovely cold the next day.

Serves 4
1 lemon, halved
2 cloves garlic, smashed
3- to 4-pound chicken, whole
1 tablespoon dried rosemary
1 tablespoon olive oil

1. Place a lemon half and the garlic cloves in the chicken's cavity.
2. Squeeze the juice from the other half of the lemon into a small bowl, and mix in the rosemary and oil.
3. Rub the mixture all over the chicken.
4. Place a clean rack or trivet in the bottom of the slow cooker, and place the chicken on top.
5. Cook on **LOW** for 8 to 10 hours, or on **HIGH** for 4 or 5.

 Tip: To smash garlic, lay clove on its side and apply heavy pressure with the side of a knife blade.

Marmalized Smoked Chicken Breast

WhamBam

A nice change from smoked ham, here, a smoked chicken breast is slow cooked in broth and marmalade. Light and lovely citrus sauce.

Serves 4

1½ pounds smoked chicken breast
½ cup chicken broth
1 cup marmalade

1. Place the chicken breast in the slow cooker, and pour the broth over the top.
2. Spread the marmalade over the chicken.
3. Cook on LOW for 4 to 6 hours, or on HIGH for 2 to 3 hours.

Tip: In supermarkets, smoked chicken breasts are often found alongside smoked hams.

The Real Deal

Funny how men and women are so different, and yet so alike. For example, if a bunch of couples are dining out in a restaurant, and a girl with big, obviously fake breasts walks by, the women in the group are unimpressed. *Hmmph*, they snort. *It doesn't count if they're not real.* The men, on the other hand, don't seem to care whether the boobs come from God or Dr. Lipenski—they're just happy they're there. Now, spin the clock ahead a few hours and the couples are standing in the parking lot. Suddenly, the well-known son of a millionaire pulls up in a top-of-the-line car. *Hmmph*, snort the men. *It doesn't count if he's not self-made.* The women don't seem to care whether the money comes from the son's blood, sweat, and tears, or his daddy's—they're just happy it's there.

Golden Cornish Hens on a Bed of Caramelized Onions

QuickEase

A culinary treasure, stolen from Greece, featuring 2 golden birds nestled in a soft bed of succulent onions. 'Tis a feast fit for the gods.

Serves 2

3 onions, sliced into ¼-inch-thick rings

¾ cup dry white wine

1 lemon, halved

2 Cornish hens

¼ cup butter, melted

2 teaspoons dried oregano

½ teaspoon dried marjoram

½ teaspoon dried thyme

¼ teaspoon dried rosemary

¼ teaspoon pepper

1. Place the onion rings in the bottom of the slow cooker, pour the wine over the onions, and squeeze the juice from half of the lemon over the top.
2. Rub the hens with the other half of lemon, and squeeze a few drops of lemon juice inside each cavity.
3. Brush the hens with the butter, and place them in the slow cooker.
4. In a small bowl, combine the remaining ingredients, and sprinkle the mixture over the hens.
5. Cook on LOW for 5 to 7 hours, or on HIGH for 2½ to 3½ hours.

 Tip: Frozen hens should be thoroughly thawed in the refrigerator before cooking.

Hunter's Partridge

33 Minutes

They say the way to a hunter's heart is through his partridge.
Show him you're game with this amazing dish.

Serves 4

2 slices bacon	3/4 cup dry red wine
2 partridges, quartered	1/2 cup water
4 potatoes, cubed	1 teaspoon pepper
3 carrots, thickly sliced	1/2 teaspoon salt
2 turnips, cubed	1/4 teaspoon
2 parsnips, sliced	dried thyme

1. In a skillet, cook the bacon until crisp; transfer the bacon to paper towels to absorb excess grease, then crumble.
2. In the same skillet, lightly brown the partridges in the bacon drippings over medium-high heat.
3. Combine the rest of the ingredients in the slow cooker.
4. Transfer the partridges to the slow cooker, tucking pieces between the vegetables, and sprinkle the bacon bits over the top.
5. Cook on LOW for 4 to 6 hours, or on HIGH for 2 to 3 hours.

 Tip: Frozen partridges are available in many supermarkets.

The Mourning After

Ever notice how a man treats you differently right after the first time you have sex with him? (Mother, if you're reading this, I'm not talking from personal experience, just from what some of my friends told me.) (None of whom you know.) (Ma, *puhlease*, I'm trying to write a book.) Your mind automatically jumps to the worst conclusions. Is he angry about something? Were you lousy? Does he think you're a tramp? According to some experts, men feel let down after the first time *not* because of any inadequacy on the woman's part, but because the thrill of the hunt is so exciting it saddens them when it's over. So, ladies, don't take it personally. Just give the guy a slap on the butt, and tell him to go hunt down breakfast. (Okay, Mother, you can open your eyes now.)

Stuffed Turkey Drums

QuickEase

Make any day feel like the holidays by serving each member of the family his or her own personal turkey drumstick packed with apricot stuffing.

Serves 4

4 turkey drumsticks	1/8 teaspoon cinnamon
2 teaspoons butter, softened	1/2 cup chicken broth
2 cups bread crumbs	1/4 cup dry white wine
1/2 cup chopped dried apricots	1/2 teaspoon pepper

1. Slip your fingers between the skin and meat on cut side of drumsticks to create "pockets."
2. Rub each drumstick with 1/2 teaspoon butter.
3. In a bowl, combine the bread crumbs, apricots, cinnamon, and just enough broth to moisten the stuffing, reserving remaining broth.
4. Stuff 1/4 of the bread crumb mixture into each drumstick's "pocket," and place the drumsticks in the slow cooker.
5. Pour the reserved broth and wine over the drumsticks, and sprinkle with pepper.
6. Cook on LOW for 8 to 10 hours, or on HIGH for 4 to 5 hours.

 Tip: Try different types of dried fruit, such as cranberries or raisins.

Turkey Casserole

QuickEase

An easy way to use up leftover turkey. Ideal for informal days when you're in the mood to let the kids chow down in front of the TV.

Serves 4

2 cups chopped cooked turkey (or chicken)

1 (10-ounce) can condensed cream of
    mushroom soup

1 (14-ounce) can chow mein noodles

1/2 cup frozen peas

1/2 cup mayonnaise

1/2 cup milk

1 onion, diced

1 celery stalk, diced

1/2 green pepper, diced

1. Combine all the ingredients in the slow cooker.
2. Cook on LOW for 3 or 4 hours.

 Tip: Leftover turkey, chicken, or chopped ham can be used in this recipe. Chow mein noodles are crispy dried noodles available in cans and packages. If using packaged noodles, measure 1³/₄ cups.

How to Pick Up a Man in a Supermarket: Part 2

Welcome back, ladies, to the second part of our class. Here we are bravely shopping in the organ section of the meat department hoping to attract a doctor. Wait a minute, darling! Don't touch that heart! Men will think you want a commitment and it'll scare them off! Okay, let's move on to poultry. Pick up a package of chicken breasts—get your hands off that enormous turkey breast, you're trying to pick up a man, not a mama's boy! All right, now, mindlessly caress the cellophane. Very good, especially the mindlessly part. Lovely, lovely, let's move on to whipped cream!

Tarragon-Dijon Turkey Breast in Wine Sauce

QuickEase

Discreetly tucked beneath the skin, a blanket of butter and tarragon moistens the turkey as it bakes in a creamy white wine sauce.

Serves 4

2-pound turkey breast
1/4 cup butter, softened
1 tablespoon dried tarragon
1 teaspoon Dijon mustard

1 (10-ounce) can condensed
  cream of celery soup
1/4 cup dry white wine
1/2 teaspoon soy sauce

1. Slip your fingers between the skin and breast meat, creating a "pocket."
2. In a small bowl, mix together the butter, tarragon, and mustard.
3. Tuck most of the mixture into the "pocket" of the turkey breast, and rub the remaining mixture over the skin.
4. Place the turkey breast in the slow cooker.
5. In a bowl, mix together the soup, wine, and soy sauce, and pour over the turkey breast.
6. Cook on LOW for 6 to 8 hours, or on HIGH for 3 to 4 hours.

 Tip: Because the wine sauce is quite rich, serve it on the side so everyone can help themselves to as much—or as little—as they prefer.

Fresh Catch Fish Stew

QuickEase

*Fresh fish, sprinkled with lemon-pepper seasoning and poached
to flaky perfection, in a creamy sauce with vegetables.
Baby, you're quite the catch yourself.*

Serves 4

4 potatoes, diced
1 onion, diced
2 cloves garlic, minced
1 carrot, thinly sliced
1 celery stalk, diced
1 teaspoon dried oregano
1 (10-ounce) can condensed
   cream of potato soup

¼ cup dry white wine *or* apple
   juice
2 pounds fish fillets, cut into
   bite-size pieces
½ teaspoon lemon-pepper
   seasoning
1 cup frozen peas

1. Combine the potatoes, onion, garlic, carrot, celery, oregano, soup, and wine (or apple juice) in the slow cooker.
2. Cook on **LOW** for 4 to 6 hours, or on **HIGH** for 2 to 3 hours.
3. Sprinkle the fish with lemon-pepper seasoning and add to the slow cooker, along with the peas; cook for an additional 20 minutes on **HIGH**.

 Tip: Use whatever type of fish your angler brings home from the lake, or the supermarket.

Fast Fish Curry

WhamBam

If you're hooked on speed, why not try one of the fastest, simplest dishes in this book? Fish fillets on a bed of sliced potatoes beneath a too-easy-to-be-true curry sauce.

Serves 4

2 (19-ounce) cans sliced potatoes, rinsed and drained
2 pounds fish fillets
1 (14-ounce) can curry sauce

1. Place the potatoes, overlapping slightly, in the bottom of slow cooker, layering if necessary.
2. Lay the fish fillets on top of the potatoes, and pour curry sauce over the fish.
3. Cook on LOW for 2 to 2½ hours.

Tip: There are lots of good-quality canned curry sauces available in supermarkets and specialty food shops, so take advantage of this quick "cheat."

Something's Fishy

A few summers ago, after my first dragon boat racing practice, I came home from the lake, wet and tired. The second I walked in the door, I was hit by how fishy I smelled. So, I jumped in the shower, dried off—but afterward, could still smell the lake. Again, I showered, this time really scrubbing. But again, when I got out of the shower, the smell was still there! Then, I spotted my wet clothes on the floor. *Silly me,* I thought, and brought them to the washing machine. But after I closed the lid, *I could still smell the smell!* Fearing the worst—could the lake actually have gotten *inside* me?—I made a mad dash back to the shower. But just as I was running through the kitchen, I spotted a skillet on the stove. In it were the remains of what Hubby had made for dinner. Trout.

Clambalaya

QuickEase

A slight variation on a fabulous dish from the Deep South.
Here, tomatoes, veggies, ham, chicken, and clams stew all
day to form a spicy concoction you mix with rice.

Serves 6

2 chicken breast halves,
    boneless, skinless, cubed
1 cup cubed cooked ham
1 onion, chopped
1 celery stalk, chopped
1 green pepper, chopped
2 cloves garlic, minced
2 teaspoons dried parsley

¼ teaspoon dried thyme
¼ teaspoon cayenne
¼ teaspoon salt
¼ teaspoon pepper
1 (5-ounce) can clams, with juice
1 (14-ounce) can diced tomatoes
4 cups cooked rice, cooled

1. Combine all the ingredients *except* the rice in the slow cooker.
2. Cook on LOW for 6 to 8 hours, or on HIGH for 3 to 4 hours.
3. Add the cooked rice, and cook for an additional 10 minutes on LOW.

Tip: For traditional Jambalaya, omit the clams, add 1 cup of tomato sauce, and plenty of cooked shrimp with the rice.

Salmon Loaf

QuickEase

*Pretty and full of flavor, salmon loaf makes a lovely lunch
or light dinner. You'll be swimming in compliments.*

Serves 4

2 (7½-ounce) cans red salmon, drained,
round bones and skin removed

1 cup bread crumbs

¼ cup milk

1 egg, slightly beaten

3 tablespoons butter, melted

2 tablespoons lemon juice

1 teaspoon dried parsley

¼ teaspoon pepper

1. Spray the bottom of the slow cooker with nonstick spray.
2. In a bowl, combine all the ingredients.
3. Form the mixture into a loaf that will fit into the slow cooker, or pack it into the bottom of slow cooker to form a "pie."
4. Cook on LOW for 4 to 6 hours.

 Tip: For a fuss-free sauce, try one of the many instant dill or lemon sauces available, which taste great with salmon loaf.

Fishing for Compliments

Women say their spouses never compliment them, but men insist they do. Maybe the problem is what a man considers a compliment:

- Sounds he makes, such as belching after dinner or snoring after sex.
- Facial twitches, such as wrinkling his nose when he catches a whiff of your perfume, or raising an eyebrow upon hearing of your promotion.
- One-word responses, like if you ask him how you look in your new bikini and he answers "cold."
- Noticing your body, even if it's to tell you your butt is blocking the wide-screen TV.
- Chores he does around the house; hey, he's doing this for you.
- Just the fact that he comes home every night; after all, his old room is still waiting for him at his mother's.

Tuna-and-Ricotta-Stuffed Cannelloni

QuickEase

Elegant pasta logs stuffed with tuna and cheese, and smothered in a creamy mushroom sauce. Lovely presentation.

Serves 4
2 (7-ounce) cans tuna, drained
1½ cups ricotta cheese
2 tablespoons diced celery stalk
2 tablespoons onion, diced
¼ teaspoon pepper
⅛ teaspoon salt
2 (10-ounce) cans condensed cream of mushroom soup
20 oven-ready cannelloni
¼ cup water

1. In a bowl, mix together the tuna, ricotta cheese, celery, onion, pepper, salt, and 2 tablespoons of the soup.
2. Using a pastry bag, stuff the mixture into the cannelloni.
3. Cover the bottom of the slow cooker with ¼-inch layer of soup.
4. Add the stuffed cannelloni, stacking crosswise if necessary, and putting a bit of soup between layers so the noodles won't stick.
5. Mix the water into remaining soup, and spread over cannelloni, making sure all are covered.
6. Cook on LOW for 3 to 4 hours.

 Tip: Top this dish with your favorite tuna casserole topping, such as potato chips, cereal crumbs, or chow mein noodles.

Tuxedo Squid

33 Minutes

Seafood and tomatoes marry well in this simple yet sophisticated casserole.
Serve with plenty of bread to sop up every last drop of sauce.

Serves 4

1 onion, chopped
1 clove garlic, minced
1 tablespoon olive oil
1 pound squid rings
1 (28-ounce) can plum tomatoes,
  broken up

$^{1}/_{2}$ teaspoon dried basil
$^{1}/_{2}$ teaspoon dried oregano
$^{1}/_{4}$ teaspoon chili pepper flakes
2 cups bowtie pasta, uncooked

1. In a large skillet, cook the onion and garlic in oil over medium-high heat for 3 minutes.
2. Add the squid rings, and cook over medium-high heat until the squid is almost white; transfer squid mixture to slow cooker.
3. In the same skillet, combine the tomatoes, basil, oregano, and chili pepper flakes, and bring to a boil; transfer mixture to slow cooker.
4. Cook on LOW for 3 to 4 hours.
5. Cook the pasta according to package directions, drain, and stir pasta into slow cooker; cook for an additional 15 minutes on LOW.

 Tip: If cleaning squid makes you squeamish, ready-to-go rings are available fresh or frozen in many supermarkets.

Spicy Chickpea Casserole with Quinoa

QuickEase

The subtle nuttiness of chickpeas bathed in a spicy red tomato sauce and boosted by one of the world's most protein-rich grains creates a wholesome casserole that's big on flavor.

Serves 4
1 red pepper, chopped
1 red onion, chopped
2 carrots, thinly sliced
2 (19-ounce) cans chickpeas, drained and rinsed
1 (28-ounce) can diced tomatoes
1/3 cup quinoa, uncooked
1 bay leaf
1/2 teaspoon ground cumin
1/2 teaspoon ground coriander
1/4 teaspoon cayenne
1/4 teaspoon pepper

1. Combine all the ingredients in the slow cooker.
2. Cook on LOW for 8 to 10 hours, or on HIGH for 4 to 5 hours.
3. Remove the bay leaf, and serve.

 Tip: Quinoa (pronounced: KEEN-wa) is available in health food stores, and some supermarkets.

Mushroom and Barley Casserole with Gorgonzola

QuickEase

In this comforting casserole, pearl barley, mushrooms, onions, and butter bake beneath a blanket of crumbled Gorgonzola.

Serves 4

2 cups sliced mushrooms
1 cup pearl barley
1 onion, chopped
1/4 cup butter, melted
1 teaspoon salt

1/2 teaspoon pepper
2 cups vegetable broth
2 ounces Gorgonzola *or*
    other high-quality blue
    cheese, crumbled

1. Combine all the ingredients *except* the Gorgonzola in the slow cooker.
2. Cook on LOW for 5 to 7 hours, or on HIGH for 2 1/2 to 3 1/2 hours.
3. Stir the casserole, and sprinkle Gorgonzola on top.
4. Cook for an additional 30 minutes to 1 hour on LOW.

Tip: Gorgonzola adds a creamy richness to the dish, but other types of blue cheese may be used. If blue cheese is not to your liking, you may substitute your favorite cheese or omit cheese altogether.

Easy Chili Rice

WhamBam

Treat yourself to a dish so easy to make, it's a gift. Perfect for days when you're not sure what you want, except spare time.

Serves 4

1 (19-ounce) can red kidney beans
1/2 cup water
1 (19-ounce) can chili-style stewed tomatoes
1 cup uncooked rice

1. Drain the beans, reserving all of the liquid.
2. Combine the bean liquid with 1/2 cup of water, and pour into slow cooker, along with 1 cup of the beans (reserve the remaining beans for another use).
3. Stir the tomatoes and rice into slow cooker.
4. Cook on LOW for 4 to 6 hours.

 Tip: If chili-style tomatoes are unavailable, use regular stewed tomatoes with 2 teaspoons chili powder.

Hint Hint

Dear Hubby,

For my upcoming birthday I'd like my present to be a surprise, but to help you out, I thought I'd mention a few things I don't want. Please, no more bath stuff. I could spend the rest of my life submerged in the tub and not use up all the bubbles you've given me. And, please, no electronics. I like the equalizer thingy but I don't really understand it, and I love the wide-screen TV but I've never even held the remote control. Oh, and don't get me stuff for work. Remember the year I told you I wanted something leather? I didn't mean a briefcase. Finally, no lingerie. Whenever I wear that skimpy thing you bought me you look shocked, and I don't know if it's a good shock or a bad shock, so nothing sheer, okay? Everything else is fine.

Your Loving Wife

Wild Rice and Pecan Pilaf

33 Minutes

Pleasing to the eye as well as the palate, sautéed pecans are a mouthwatering addition to a bed of wild rice.

Serves 4

1 cup wild rice, uncooked
2 cups water
1 teaspoon vegetable bouillon powder
1 teaspoon plus 2 tablespoons butter
1/4 cup pecan pieces

1. Combine the rice, water, vegetable bouillon powder, and 1 teaspoon butter in the slow cooker.
2. Cook on LOW for 6 to 8 hours.
3. In a small skillet, cook the pecans in the remaining butter over medium heat for 4 minutes; stir into slow cooker, and serve.

 Tip: Recipe may be increased, but always keep water to rice ratio at 2:1. To keep shelled pecans as fresh as possible, store in an airtight container or buy in small quantities as needed.

Bulgur and Mixed Bean Chili

33 Minutes

After spending hours together, grains, legumes, and spices come together in a zippy explosion of flavor that easily rivals any meat-based chili.

Serves 4

2 onions, chopped
2 cloves garlic, minced
1/2 green pepper, chopped
1/2 red pepper, chopped
1 tablespoon oil
1 tablespoon chili powder
1 tablespoon ground cumin
1 teaspoon dried oregano

1/4 teaspoon cayenne
1 (28-ounce) can ground or
   crushed tomatoes
1 cup water
1/2 cup bulgur
1 (19-ounce) can mixed beans,
   rinsed and drained

1. In a large skillet, cook the onions, garlic, and peppers in oil over medium-high heat for 3 minutes.
2. Stir in the chili powder, cumin, oregano, and cayenne, and cook over medium-high heat for 3 minutes.
3. Add the tomatoes and water, and cook over medium-high heat for an additional 3 minutes.
4. Transfer mixture to slow cooker, and stir in the bulgur and the beans.
5. Cook on LOW for 4 to 6 hours, or on HIGH for 2 to 3 hours.

 Tip: Bulgur, a cracked wheat, is rich in protein and can be used in place of meat in many recipes.

Cheese Sandwich Pudding

QuickEase

Cheese sandwiches in the slow cooker? You betcha. Thanks to the addition of eggs, milk, and butter, this makes a hot and wholesome family favorite!

Serves 4

8 slices stale white bread

1/4 cup butter

4 slices processed cheese

4 eggs

1 cup milk

1/2 cup grated Cheddar cheese

1. Assemble 4 cheese sandwiches the usual way, buttering both pieces of bread.
2. Cut into quarters, diagonally, and place the triangles crust side down in the slow cooker, stacking if necessary.
3. In a bowl, beat together the eggs and milk for 1 minute, and pour the mixture over the cheese sandwiches, making sure all are covered.
4. Sprinkle grated Cheddar cheese over the top.
5. Cook on LOW for 4 to 6 hours, or on HIGH for 2 to 3 hours.

Tip: If you have only fresh bread on hand, leave slices uncovered on the counter overnight and then assemble the sandwiches in the morning.

Chef EGGstraordinaire?

Why do men get so much glory for making breakfast? Is it just me, or don't you get sick of everyone patting your man on the back just because he flips a few eggs over easy? If your husband is like mine, it's not like he gets up early every weekday and painstakingly prepares and lays out a fabulous feast. Most of my girlfriends say their husbands don't even cook breakfast once a weekend! And yet, for some reason, the fact that a guy whips out his spatula when he's in the mood earns him the status of Chef Extraordinaire. Give me a break. If a woman only knew how to cook eggs and she did so only occasionally, people would call it a weakness. But for a guy? That's a *specialty*.

Saucy Vegetables

9 different types of vegetables, layered on top of one another, then smothered in a tomato sauce that includes lots of herbs and spices. Tasty, and very impressive.

Serves 6

4 potatoes, cubed	1½ cups tomato sauce
1 red onion, sliced	1½ teaspoons soy sauce
2 parsnips, sliced	1 teaspoon dry mustard
1 red pepper, sliced	1 teaspoon chili powder
½ zucchini, sliced	1 teaspoon dried parsley
1 cup frozen peas *or* corn	1 teaspoon dried basil
10 button mushrooms	¼ teaspoon dried thyme
10 broccoli flowerets	¼ teaspoon cinnamon
6 string beans, thickly sliced	⅛ teaspoon dried sage

1. Layer the potatoes, red onion, parsnips, red pepper, zucchini, peas (or corn), mushrooms, broccoli, and string beans, in that order, in the slow cooker.
2. In a bowl, mix together the remaining ingredients, and pour over vegetables.
3. Cook on LOW for 8 to 10 hours, or on HIGH for 4 to 5 hours.

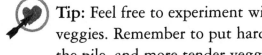 **Tip:** Feel free to experiment with other types of fresh and frozen veggies. Remember to put hard vegetables toward the bottom of the pile, and more tender veggies toward the top.

Ratatouille

QuickEase

Guests won't say no to this classic French stew in which eggplant, zucchini, onion, red pepper, and herbs wallow in a tangy tomato sauce.

Serves 4

1 eggplant, sliced
2 zucchini, sliced
1 red pepper, chopped
1 onion, coarsely chopped
2 cloves garlic, minced
$1/3$ cup grated Parmesan cheese
1 (28-ounce) can diced tomatoes
$1/2$ teaspoon dried basil
$1/4$ teaspoon dried oregano
$1/4$ teaspoon dried parsley

1. To remove the bitter juices, sprinkle the sliced eggplant with salt and let drain in a colander for 20 minutes; rinse, and pat dry.
2. Combine all the ingredients in the slow cooker.
3. Cook on LOW for 6 to 8 hours.

 Tip: For a more substantial ratatouille, include a few cubed potatoes in the mix.

Mediterranean Stew over Couscous

33 Minutes

*Members of the squash family get together in this spicy stew
and couscous entrée. A wonderful aroma.*

Serves 6

1 eggplant, cubed
2 zucchini, cubed
1 butternut squash, cubed
1 onion, chopped
1 tomato, chopped
1 carrot, sliced
1 clove garlic, minced
1/3 cup raisins
1 (14-ounce) can tomato sauce
1/4 cup water

1 teaspoon vegetable broth powder
1/2 teaspoon ground cumin
1/2 teaspoon turmeric
1/4 teaspoon red pepper flakes
1/4 teaspoon cinnamon
1/4 teaspoon paprika
3 cups vegetable broth
1/2 teaspoon salt
2 cups couscous

1. Sprinkle the cubed eggplant with salt and let drain in a colander for 20 minutes; rinse, pat dry, and add to slow cooker.
2. Combine all the remaining ingredients *except* the broth, salt, and couscous in the slow cooker.
3. Cook on **LOW** for 6 to 8 hours, or on **HIGH** for 3 to 4 hours.
4. In a saucepan, combine the broth and salt, and bring to a boil; stir in the couscous, cover, and remove from heat.
5. Let the couscous sit for 5 minutes; then fluff with a fork, and serve with stew over the top.

 Tip: While a little more expensive, precut squash is a real time-saver.

Vegetable Bin Curry

33 Minutes

For days when your veggie bin is stuffed with produce
you have absolutely no idea what to do with.

Serves 4

8 cups assorted fresh
    vegetables, cut into
    bite-size pieces
1 (19-ounce) can chickpeas,
    rinsed and drained
1 onion, chopped
1 clove garlic, minced

1 tablespoon oil
1 tablespoon curry powder
1/2 teaspoon ground cumin
1/4 teaspoon red pepper flakes
1/4 teaspoon salt
3/4 cup vegetable broth

1. Place the vegetables and chickpeas in the slow cooker.
2. In a skillet, cook the onion and garlic in oil over medium-high heat for 3 minutes.
3. Stir in the curry powder, cumin, red pepper flakes, and salt, and cook for 2 minutes, stirring constantly.
4. Stir in the broth and bring to a boil; reduce heat, and let cook for an additional 2 minutes.
5. Transfer mixture to slow cooker, and stir.
6. Cook on LOW for 6 to 10 hours, or on HIGH for 3 to 5 hours, depending on types of vegetables (root vegetables take longer).

 Tip: Don't hesitate to use vegetables a tad past their prime—in this lively mixture, no one will notice.

Vegan Cassoulet

QuickEase

Simple. Wholesome. And bursting with flavor. Every chef has her own way of preparing cassoulet; here is yours.

Serves 4

1 (19-ounce) can haricot beans, rinsed and
  drained
1 (19-ounce) can black beans, rinsed and drained
2 carrots, sliced
1 celery stalk, chopped
1 onion, chopped
1 garlic clove, minced
1 bay leaf
1 (14-ounce) can diced tomatoes
1/4 cup dry white wine
1/2 teaspoon brown sugar
1/4 teaspoon thyme
1/4 teaspoon salt
1/4 teaspoon pepper

1. Combine all the ingredients in the slow cooker.
2. Cook on LOW for 6 to 8 hours, or on HIGH
   for 3 to 4 hours. Remove the bay leaf, and serve.

 Tip: Throw in whatever you have on hand in the way of beans, such as kidney, lima, or string beans.

Fridge Magnet?

There's something wrong with my fridge. It's as if it has some magnetic hold over the food that's put inside it. The other day I watched my son pour himself a glass of orange juice, see that there were only a few drops left in the pitcher, and then stick it back in the fridge. Yesterday, I saw my daughter take a carrot from the vegetable crisper, note that it was rotten, and toss it back in the bin! Today, my husband took out a carton of sour cream, lifted its lid, and muttered the words *Eww . . . mold.* What did he do next? He stuffed it back in the fridge, slammed the door, and walked away disgusted! Time and again, I've told everyone that a fridge can only keep things cold; it has no restorative powers. And yet, this senseless behavior continues. *Hmm.* Maybe there's something wrong with my family?

Spaghetti Squash and Tomato Balls

QuickEase

What looks like spaghetti and meatballs but contains no pasta or meat?
In this clever dish, cherry tomatoes sit on top of a pile of shredded
squash—a dead-ringer for strands of spaghetti.

Serves 2

1/2 spaghetti squash, unpeeled	1/3 cup bottled spicy pasta sauce
1/2 cup water	2 tablespoons butter (optional)
1 1/2 cups cherry tomatoes	1/4 cup grated Parmesan cheese

1. Remove the pulp and seeds from the squash, and place the squash in the slow cooker, cut-side up, and pour the water around it.
2. Cut a square piece of cheesecloth about twice as big as the squash's cavity, and set it across the cavity.
3. With a sharp knife, make a small slit in each cherry tomato, and then place them on top of the cheesecloth. Pour the pasta sauce over the tomatoes.
4. Tie the corners of the cheesecloth together to form a sack.
5. Cook on LOW for 4 to 6 hours.
6. Transfer the sack of tomatoes to a bowl, remove the squash, and use a fork to scrape the squash lengthwise to form strands.
7. Pile the squash strands on a platter and dollop with butter, if desired.
8. Remove tomatoes from cheesecloth, pour on top of squash, and sprinkle with Parmesan cheese.

 Tip: Cut squash lengthwise. When buying squash, remember that one half must fit in your slow cooker!

Spaghetti Puttanesca

QuickEase

A spicy Italian sauce you let brew for hours before adding the pasta. Seductively easy.

Serves 4

1 (28-ounce) can plum tomatoes, broken up
2 tablespoons tomato paste
2 cloves garlic, minced
1 onion, chopped
10 black olives, pitted, halved
1 tablespoon capers, rinsed
1 teaspoon dried basil
1 teaspoon dried parsley
$1/2$ teaspoon red pepper flakes
1 cup spaghetti, uncooked, broken into
    1-inch pieces

1. Combine all the ingredients *except* the spaghetti in the slow cooker.
2. Cook on LOW for 6 to 8 hours, or on HIGH for 3 to 4 hours.
3. Stir in the spaghetti and cook for an additional 30 minutes on HIGH.

Tip: If fish is agreeable to you, add 1 (2-ounce) tin of chopped anchovies for a truly authentic flavor.

Speaking of Italian . . .

It may surprise you to learn that *Spaghetti Puttanesca* means "whore's spaghetti." There are different theories as to how the dish got its name. Some think it's because the ladies of the evening used to prepare this sauce and let it simmer for hours while they were at work. That way, when they got home, a delicious meal was ready and waiting. Others believe the dish got its name because of its wonderful aroma. Just a whiff of the sauce was so alluring it would bring customers to the woman's door! Regardless of its origin, there is definitely something fetching about the name. If you don't believe me, next time your hubby calls and asks what's for dinner, tell him what you're having—in English. You may be surprised how quickly he comes home.

3-Cheese and Spinach Cannelloni

QuickEase

*Thanks to good-quality bottled pasta sauce and oven-ready pasta,
this fabulous Italian classic is possible in your slow cooker.
First you stuff the pasta . . . then you stuff yourself.*

Serves 6

1 (10-ounce) package frozen
    chopped spinach, thawed,
    drained
1 cup ricotta cheese
4 ounces cream cheese, softened

¼ cup grated Parmesan cheese
1 egg, beaten
¼ teaspoon nutmeg
20 oven-ready cannelloni
2 cups pasta sauce

1. In a bowl, mix together the spinach, ricotta cheese, cream cheese, Parmesan cheese, egg, and nutmeg.
2. Using a pastry bag, or by hand, stuff the cannelloni with mixture.
3. Cover the bottom of the slow cooker with ¼-inch layer of pasta sauce.
4. Place the cannelloni side by side in the slow cooker, stacking crosswise if necessary, and putting a bit of sauce between each layer so the noodles won't stick.
5. Pour remaining sauce over the cannelloni, making sure all are covered.
6. Cook on LOW for 3 to 4 hours.

Tip: To make your own pastry bag: Take a medium-size freezer or sandwich bag, fill it with cheese-spinach mixture, and cut a hole about the size of a nickel in one of the bottom corners.

Red Pepper and Tomato Pasta Toss

QuickEase

A mildly spiced medley of red peppers, tomatoes, zucchini, and red onions ready to toss with your favorite pasta.

Serves 4

1 red pepper, chopped
1 zucchini, chopped
1 red onion, chopped
2 cloves garlic, minced
1 (28-ounce) can diced tomatoes
3 teaspoons tomato paste
1 teaspoon brown sugar
1/2 teaspoon dried oregano
1/2 teaspoon dried basil
1/4 teaspoon crushed red pepper flakes

1. Combine the red pepper, zucchini, red onion, and garlic in the slow cooker.
2. In a bowl, combine the remaining ingredients, and stir into slow cooker.
3. Cook on LOW for 6 to 8 hours, or on HIGH for 3 to 4 hours; serve tossed with cooked pasta.

 Tip: If you prefer a thicker sauce, turn slow cooker to HIGH and remove cover. Let cook an additional 30 minutes on HIGH.

How to Tell if Your Man Is Seeing Red

Men show no emotions at the best of times, so it's hard to tell if they're angry. To determine whether your man is being his normal sullen self or giving you the Silent Treatment, scream WHAZZUP in his ear. If he flinches and looks away, he's mad, but if there's no reaction, check his pulse—he may just be dead. To determine whether your man is driving dangerously just for fun or if he's giving you the Drive Like a Maniac Treatment, check for veins popping out of his neck. If they are, drop whatever subject you've been pressing. To determine whether your man is being lazy as usual or if he's giving you the Don't Lift a Finger to Help Treatment, pile all the dirty dishes on his side of the bed. If he gets excited like you've dreamed up a new kinky sex game, don't worry, he may be crazy—but he's not mad.

Green Vegetable Pasta Sauce with Asiago

Tender asparagus spears, sweet peas, and lima beans unite in a tarragon vegetable sauce enriched with a splash of cream and a sprinkle of Asiago.

Serves 6

$^1\!/_2$ pound asparagus spears	1 teaspoon dried tarragon	1 teaspoon butter
1 cup frozen lima beans	1 teaspoon dried parsley	$^1\!/_4$ cup cream
1 cup frozen peas	$^1\!/_4$ teaspoon salt	$^1\!/_4$ cup grated Asiago cheese
1 small onion, chopped	$^1\!/_2$ cup vegetable broth	$^1\!/_4$ teaspoon salt
		1 teaspoon lemon juice

1. Remove and discard the tough ends of the asparagus; cut spears into 1-inch pieces, and reserve tips.
2. Combine the asparagus pieces with the lima beans, peas, onion, tarragon, parsley, $^1\!/_4$ teaspoon salt, broth, and butter in the slow cooker, and place reserved asparagus tips on top.
3. Cook on LOW for $2^1\!/_2$ to $3^1\!/_2$ hours.
4. Drain the vegetables, setting aside the broth, asparagus tips, and about 1 cup of the other vegetables.
5. Transfer the remaining vegetables to a blender or food processor, add $^1\!/_4$ cup of the reserved broth, and purée until smooth.
6. Transfer the puréed mixture to the slow cooker, and add the asparagus tips, reserved whole vegetables, cream, Asiago, and salt; cook for an additional 20 minutes on LOW. Stir in the lemon juice, and serve.

 Tip: This sauce looks lovely over tricolor pasta.

Pasta Primavera

33 Minutes

Rotini pasta in a garlicky cream sauce accented with broccoli, cauliflower, peas, carrots, and red peppers. A refreshing taste of spring regardless of the season.

Serves 4

3 cups uncooked rotini pasta
1 cup frozen broccoli and
   cauliflower
1 cup frozen peas
1 red pepper, diced
1 carrot, thinly sliced
1 clove garlic, minced

1 (13-ounce) can evaporated milk
1/2 cup milk
1 tablespoon cornstarch
1/4 teaspoon salt
1 cup shredded mozzarella cheese
1 tablespoon butter

1. Cook the pasta until not quite done, and drain.
2. Meanwhile, combine the broccoli and cauliflower, peas, red pepper, carrot, and garlic in the slow cooker.
3. In a bowl, combine the evaporated milk, milk, cornstarch, salt, and cheese.
4. Transfer the pasta to the slow cooker, stir in the milk mixture, and dollop with butter.
5. Cook on LOW for 3 to 4 hours.

 Tip: Try different types of frozen veggies, such as international blends.

Vegging Out Lasagna

33 Minutes

A lazy lasagna of flavored tofu, veggies, pasta, and sauce. Here's a tasty, healthful casserole to leave the family the next time you're spending the evening out.

Serves 4

1 onion, chopped

1 clove garlic, minced

2 tablespoons oil

1 cup herb-flavored firm tofu, crumbled

4 cups bottled pasta sauce

9 lasagna noodles, oven-ready type, uncooked

1 cup shredded mozzarella cheese

1. In a large skillet, cook the onion and garlic in oil over medium-high heat for 3 minutes.
2. Stir in the tofu and cook over medium-high heat for an additional 4 minutes, stirring frequently.
3. Stir in the sauce and cook over medium-high heat for an additional 3 minutes.
4. Break each lasagna noodle into approximately 4 pieces, and add to sauce mixture, stirring to ensure each piece is coated.
5. Transfer mixture to slow cooker, and sprinkle cheese on top.
6. Cook on LOW for 2 to 3 hours.

 Tip: If you're strapped for time, omit the browning stage, and simply combine onion, garlic, tofu, sauce, and noodles in slow cooker, top with cheese, and cook.

Eggplants with Caper-and-Olive Stuffing

QuickEase

*A dish that brings together the traditional eggplant-tomato
combo with a surprising bite, courtesy of the capers.*

Serves 4

2 eggplants, halved crosswise

20 black olives, pitted, chopped

2 tablespoons capers, rinsed and
   drained

1 cup bread crumbs

2 tablespoons grated Parmesan
   cheese

1/4 teaspoon pepper

1 cup tomato sauce

1. Using a teaspoon, or melon baller, scoop out each eggplant half, leaving shells about 1/4-inch thick. (Reserve scooped-out eggplant for another use.)
2. Slice off a bit of the bottom of each eggplant half so it can rest upright without toppling over.
3. Sprinkle the eggplant shells with salt and let drain in a colander for 20 minutes; rinse and pat dry.
4. In a bowl, combine the olives, capers, bread crumbs, Parmesan, pepper, and 1/4 cup of the tomato sauce.
5. Stuff the mixture into the eggplant halves, and place upright in slow cooker.
6. Pour the remaining tomato sauce over the eggplants.
7. Cook on LOW for 3 to 4 hours.
8. Slice the eggplants crosswise into 1-inch rings, and serve.

 Tip: Choose shorter, fatter eggplants for this recipe.

Fruit-and-Nut-Stuffed Red Cabbage Bowls

33 Minutes

A stunning presentation that features edible red cabbage bowls
brimming with a raisin-pear-walnut stuffing.

Serves 2

1 head red cabbage
1 ⅓ cups vegetable broth
1 cup bread crumbs
1 pear, diced
½ cup raisins

¼ cup chopped walnuts
½ teaspoon dried thyme
½ teaspoon dried parsley
1 teaspoon butter

1. To prepare the cabbage: Carefully remove a few leaves and set them aside; then cut the cabbage in half, crosswise. Next, set the half without the core on a work surface, and gently pull away inner layers of cabbage, leaving a ½-inch–thick shell. Next, using a sharp knife, remove the core from the other half; then pull away the inner layers of cabbage. Place the reserved cabbage leaves inside the cabbage half to cover the hole.

2. In a bowl, combine ⅓ cup of the broth, the bread crumbs, pear, raisins, walnuts, thyme, and parsley; stuff the mixture into the cabbage "bowls."

3. Dollop each cabbage bowl with ½ teaspoon butter.

4. Carefully transfer the cabbage bowls to the slow cooker, stacking askew, if necessary.

5. Pour the remaining broth around the rims of the bowls to moisten the cabbage, but do not soak the stuffing.

6. Cook on LOW for 4 hours, or until the cabbage is tender.

 Tip: Don't worry—bowl preparation is not as hard as it seems!

Companions—Side Dishes

185

Quick, think about the last time you saw a woman in a lovely outfit but the entire effect was ruined because she had the wrong shoes. One small oversight, and suddenly, Little Miss Fashion Statement looks like a hag. The same is true of dinner. When a fabulous entrée is forced to share the plate with a blob of gooey mashed potatoes and a heap of lukewarm peas, the whole damn dinner is reduced to the Saturday Night Special at the diner of some 1-horse town.

A side dish is supposed to do more than just take up space. It should complement the main course without overshadowing it, provide instant visual stimulus, and tantalize the palate with taste and textural variety (hey, no one said it was easy being a cob of corn).

Preparing your side dish in a slow cooker provides many advantages. For example, say you're stuck doing the Thanksgiving meal and your oven is stuffed with turkey, and every burner on your stove is bubbling over. Why not prepare Glazed Ginger Carrots in the crock? Or, for your next barbecue, why cram everything on the grill when the slow cooker makes Open Jacket Potatoes with Lemon and Capers just heavenly?

As an added perk, slow cookers eliminate the timing problem thing. You know, that sinking feeling you get when the beef is still bloody but the string beans are done? Do you nuke the beef so it tastes like a shoe? Or keep boiling the beans and act like you intended purée? If you're lucky, that sinking feeling will turn into out-and-out nausea and all your guests will have to go home! Or, you can avoid this crisis altogether by doing the side dish in the slow cooker, knowing it will hold an extra hour or so if you screw up the meat.

Speaking of screwing up, I will remind you that it is almost impossible to do so in your slow cooker. Low, even temperatures, long cooking times—baby, not even you can burn the beets! And once you've tried a few of the recipes in this section, flip through the Vegetarian ones in Main Courses. Many of the lovely meatless entrées listed there do double-duty as sumptuous side dishes.

On a final note, may I be so bold as to suggest you purchase more than 1 slow cooker? (I have 5, tee-hee!) That way, you can do your main course in 1, your side dish in the other, and you can go off gallivanting for the day! Not that I'm off gallivanting per se . . . but, you may choose to.

Open Jacket Potatoes with Lemon and Capers

QuickEase

Pried-open, baby new potatoes, slow cooked in a buttery lemon sauce spiked with the sharpness of capers. Magnificently Mediterranean.

Serves 4

16 small new potatoes, unpeeled	1 teaspoon Dijon mustard
16 capers, rinsed, drained	1 teaspoon lemon juice
2 tablespoons olive oil	1/4 teaspoon salt
2 tablespoons butter, melted	1/4 teaspoon pepper

1. Slice the potatoes in half, but not completely through, so the potato "jacket" remains partially intact.
2. Insert 1 caper into the slit of each potato to hold it slightly open.
3. Transfer potatoes to slow cooker.
4. In a bowl, combine the olive oil, butter, Dijon mustard, lemon juice, salt, and pepper; pour the mixture over the top of the potatoes, stirring gently to ensure the potatoes are coated.
5. Cook on LOW for 8 to 10 hours, or on HIGH for 4 to 5 hours.

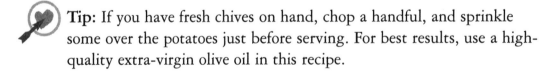

Tip: If you have fresh chives on hand, chop a handful, and sprinkle some over the potatoes just before serving. For best results, use a high-quality extra-virgin olive oil in this recipe.

Potatoes Paprika

QuickEase

Cream cheese and paprika give ordinary mashed potatoes both depth and kick. Not too heavy, not too light—just right.

Serves 4
5 potatoes, cubed
1/2 cup chicken broth
1 teaspoon paprika
1/4 teaspoon pepper
4 ounces cream cheese, cubed
Salt to taste (optional)

1. Place the potatoes and broth in the slow cooker.
2. Sprinkle with paprika and pepper.
3. Cook on LOW for 8 to 10 hours, or on HIGH for 4 to 5 hours.
4. Stir in the cream cheese, and mash thoroughly.
5. Sprinkle with salt, if desired.

 Tip: Paprika can be mild, strong, or hot depending on the type of red pepper it's made from. Either Spanish or Hungarian paprika can be used in this recipe, but if you like heat, look for a Hungarian hot paprika and adjust the quantity according to taste. Also, because different types and brands have different flavors, purchase paprika in small quantities until you find your favorite.

Scalloped Red Potatoes

QuickEase

In this upscale version of scalloped potatoes, red potatoes and red onions turn tender beneath a canopy of mushrooms and cheese.

Serves 6

2 pounds red potatoes, unpeeled, thinly sliced
1 cup water
1 teaspoon hot pepper sauce
1/2 teaspoon cream of tartar
1 large red onion, sliced
1/3 cup flour
1 teaspoon salt

1/4 teaspoon white pepper
1 1/2 cup shredded white Cheddar cheese
3 tablespoons butter
1 (10-ounce) can condensed cream of mushroom soup
1/4 teaspoon dried dill

1. Place the potato slices, water, hot pepper sauce, and cream of tartar in a large bowl; let soak for 5 minutes, then drain.
2. Spray the slow cooker with nonstick spray, and then layer half the potatoes on the bottom of the slow cooker.
3. Add the red onions, and sprinkle with half of the flour. Add the salt, pepper, 1 cup of the cheese, and dollop with half of the butter. Layer the remaining potatoes, red onions, flour, and butter, and pour the soup over the top.
4. Cook on LOW for 8 to 10 hours, or on HIGH for 4 to 5 hours.
5. Sprinkle the remaining cheese and the dill on top, and cook for an additional 20 minutes on LOW.

 Tip: Great alongside any grilled meat, this is a lovely side dish that won't heat up the kitchen or take up precious grill space at a barbecue.

Lemon Rice with Lima Beans and Artichokes

QuickEase

A fragrant Greek dish that infuses white rice with the classic lemon-dill combo. Lima beans and artichoke quarters add taste and textural pleasure.

Serves 4
1 (14-ounce) can artichoke quarters, drained
1 cup frozen lima beans
1¼ cups rice
1 onion, chopped
1 tablespoon butter
1 tablespoon lemon juice
½ teaspoon lemon zest
½ teaspoon dried dill
¼ teaspoon dried parsley
¼ teaspoon salt
¼ teaspoon pepper
2 cups boiling water

1. Combine all the ingredients in the slow cooker.
2. Cook on LOW for 2½ to 4 hours.

 Tip: To obtain zest, rub a lemon against the smallest holes of a grater, collecting only the yellow part.

Wild Rice and Smoked Turkey Pilaf

QuickEase

A festive pilaf of wild rice, smoked turkey, and bites of tang thanks to the cranberries.

Serves 4

½ cup wild rice, uncooked
½ cup dried cranberries
3 ounces smoked turkey breast, chopped
1 teaspoon butter
¼ teaspoon nutmeg
¼ teaspoon pepper
¼ teaspoon salt
1¼ cups chicken broth

1. Combine all the ingredients in the slow cooker.
2. Cook on LOW for 6 to 8 hours.

 Tip: Wild rice is not rice at all, but rather the seed of an aquatic grass. It is dark brown or black, and has a nutty flavor. Because it's way more expensive than regular white rice, serve it on special occasions or to someone special. Along with salad and soup, Wild Rice and Smoked Turkey Pilaf can be served as a main course for 2.

My Christmas To-Do List

1. Beg Hubby to put up outdoor lights.
2. Find last year's decorations; if can't find or look passé, buy more.
3. Decorate tree, house, and gingerbread house.
4. Learn how to bake gingerbread house.
5. Buy gifts for everyone alive on family tree, everyone who teaches kids anything, and everyone who delivers anything to our door.
6. Wrap presents, mail out-of-towners early so less expensive; drop off presents to in-town people so don't have to have them over like last year.
7. Stock up on food and booze, just in case.
8. Sew wise man costume for school play; make something that looks like myrrh.
9. Find out what myrrh is.
10. Maintain cheerful holiday spirit even when wearing black velour pants.
11. Maintain cheerful holiday spirit even knowing that next spring when begging Hubby to take down outdoor lights, he'll complain it's such a *hassle*.

Red Rice and Beans

QuickEase

Spicy tomatoes paint the rice red in this meatless dish reminiscent of the Louisiana favorite.

Serves 4

1 onion, chopped
1 green pepper, chopped
$1/2$ teaspoon salt
$1/2$ teaspoon chili powder
$1/4$ teaspoon garlic powder
$1/4$ teaspoon pepper
$1/4$ teaspoon cayenne
1 (19-ounce) can red kidney beans, rinsed and drained
1 cup rice, uncooked
1 cup boiling water
1 (28-ounce) can diced tomato

1. Combine all the ingredients in the slow cooker.
2. Cook on LOW for 3 to 5 hours.

Tip: Remember to use long-grain white rice in this recipe, as it holds up best. This is a relatively mild dish, so if you're after more kick, up the quantity of cayenne.

French-Canadian Baked Beans

QuickEase

*While you sleep, dried beans soak to regain their moisture so they're
ready to bake in the morning. Whether gobbled down at the
dinner table or the campfire, these are delicious.*

Serves 6

2 cups dried navy *or* haricot beans

½ pound salt pork, chopped

1 onion, chopped

3 tablespoons brown sugar

3 tablespoons molasses

2 tablespoons ketchup

1 teaspoon salt

½ teaspoon dry mustard

1 cup water

1. To prepare the beans: Spread the beans out on a baking sheet or
   other flat surface and remove stones and any beans that are shriveled
   or cracked. Transfer to a colander or sieve, and rinse thoroughly with
   cold water. Soak overnight in 6 cups of water, drain, and rinse in
   very hot water.
2. Transfer the drained beans to the slow cooker and add the salt pork.
3. In a bowl, combine the onion, brown sugar, molasses, ketchup, salt,
   mustard, and water, and pour into slow cooker.
4. Cook on LOW for 8 to 10 hours.

 Tip: If there isn't enough liquid to cover the beans, add a bit
more water.

Balsamic Beets

QuickEase

Among the prettiest of vegetables is the common beet. Here, beets are slow cooked in a sweet glaze to bring out their deep red beauty.

Serves 4

1 pound small whole beets, peeled
$\frac{1}{4}$ cup vegetable *or* beef broth
2 tablespoons balsamic vinegar
1 tablespoon sugar
$\frac{1}{4}$ teaspoon salt
$\frac{1}{4}$ teaspoon pepper

1. Place the beets and broth in the slow cooker.
2. In a small bowl, combine the balsamic vinegar, sugar, salt, and pepper, and pour over the beets.
3. Cook on LOW for 8 to 10 hours, or on HIGH for 4 to 5.

 Tip: To cook beets more quickly, cut them into cubes before placing them in the slow cooker and cook for 5 or 6 hours on LOW.

The Helpful Shopper

My family won't go shopping with me. They say I'm too embarrassing. See, when I'm in a clothing store, I enjoy offering my opinion to people trying things on. I know they instinctively trust me because lots of times they ask me to get them another size. And if I'm in a video store, I like telling perfect strangers about a movie I've enjoyed. I know it saves them money, because lots of times they put the video back, saying they feel like they've seen it already. In supermarkets I truly blossom. Anytime I deliver an impromptu speech about some product, the more passionate I get, the more shoppers gather around! One time in the bakery section, I was on such a roll someone called management! Anyway, it's a shame about my family. I've offered to teach them how to work through their hostile feelings, but they refuse my help.

Caramelized Shallots

WhamBam

*A mainstay in northern France, shallots are a tasty, pick-me-up
to grilled beef, lamb, or pork at your next barbecue.*

Serves 4

20 shallots, peeled, thinly sliced
1 tablespoon olive oil
2 teaspoons balsamic vinegar

1. Combine the shallots and oil in the slow
   cooker.
2. Cook on LOW for 2 to 3 hours.
3. Drizzle the balsamic vinegar over the top,
   and cook for an additional 10 minutes
   on LOW.

Tip: Shallots are like a cross between
garlic and onions. They are the same
shape as a big clove of garlic, with red-
dish-brown papery skin. Look for
smooth, firm shallots that haven't begun
to sprout, and keep them stored in a
cool, dry place. To peel shallots: Cut off
both ends, and make a slit in the skin
top to bottom. Roll the shallot around to
loosen the skin before peeling it off.

Think Before You Thank

Why is it that my husband gets all
the glory when we have a backyard
barbecue? Oh sure, he stands over
the grill flipping steaks for 15 minutes, say, but don't people realize
who's done everything else? Like,
who do they think painstakingly
chopped the fresh parsley and
hunted down the exotic vinegar for
that delightful marinade? And who
do they think stayed up half the
night boiling, peeling, and stuffing
deviled eggs? Do people think those
divine little cocktail napkins that so
perfectly match the outdoor table-
ware grow on trees? Do they think
it's easy to find a string of patio
lanterns shaped like chili peppers on
sale? I mean, do they really believe
Mr. Barbecue Pants went to all the
trouble of renting long wooden
tables with real tablecloths so they
don't have to eat off their hairy
knees? Think before you thank,
people. You're welcome.

Fennel with Parmesan

33 Minutes

Fabulous fennel lies beneath a coating of butter, bread crumbs, and Parmesan. Simple yet elegant.

Serves 4
4 fennel bulbs, sliced
Water to cover
1 tablespoon butter, melted
$1/2$ cup bread crumbs
$1/4$ cup grated Parmesan cheese

1. Boil the fennel slices in water for 5 minutes, drain well, and transfer to slow cooker.
2. Mix together the butter, bread crumbs, and Parmesan, and sprinkle the mixture on top of the fennel.
3. Cook on LOW for 4 to 6 hours.

 Tip: Fennel is famous for its licorice-like tasting bulb, which can be eaten raw, boiled, sautéed, or braised. Most people discard the stems, but you can throw them in a broth for extra flavor. The feathery leaves are often used as garnish for seafood salad or to add flavor to sauces. To slice fennel, cut off the stems with leaves, and the root end. Slice the bulb from top to bottom into $1/4$-inch slices.

Corn-on-the-Cob-in-the-Crock

WhamBam

It's the one vegetable kids love! Here, cobs of fresh corn are basted in parsley and butter, and slow cooked to preserve their sweet taste and nutrients.

Serves 4

1/2 cup butter, melted
1 teaspoon dried parsley
6 corncobs, cleaned, halved

1. Place a small ramekin filled with water in the center of your slow cooker.
2. Mix together the butter and parsley, and, using a pastry brush, brush each cob with the butter mixture; place the cobs in the slow cooker, surrounding the ramekin.
3. Cook on LOW for 2 to 2 1/2 hours.

 Tip: For spicy corn-on-the-cob, add 1/2 teaspoon or so of hot pepper flakes to the butter and parsley mixture.

The Sleepover from Hell

4 P.M.   Parents drop off little Johnny. Hide my surprise. Thought sleepovers start after supper. Feed him corn-on-the-cob.

8 P.M.   Johnny and my son fighting. Run to video store to get another movie.

1 A.M.   Johnny crying 'cause my son keeps hitting him with pillow. Separate boys.

6 A.M.   Kids awake. Feed them waffles. Maple syrup fight.

10 A.M. Johnny's parents not here. Call twice. No answer.

1 P.M.   Parents still not here. Wonder if they're in an accident. Hubby asks why Johnny is still here.

3 P.M.   Hubby says to throw Johnny in car and he'll drive him home. *No, I protest. What will people think?*

4 P.M.   Johnny and my son not speaking. Me and Hubby not speaking.

5 P.M.   Johnny's parents arrive, happy and refreshed. Johnny says: *Thanks for having me.* Hubby quips: *We didn't have you; your parents did. Obviously, you've been here too long.*

5:01 P.M. Vow no more sleepovers.

Glazed Ginger Carrots

QuickEase

Tender baby carrots dripping with sweetness and a breath of ginger. Suitable alongside almost any main course.

Serves 4
4 cups baby carrots
2 tablespoons butter, melted
1/4 cup honey
1 teaspoon ground ginger

1. Combine the carrots and butter in the slow cooker.
2. In a bowl, mix together the honey and ginger, and pour over the carrots.
3. Cook on LOW for 4 to 6 hours, or on HIGH for 2 to 3 hours.

 Tip: For an even prettier presentation, sprinkle with chopped fresh parsley before serving. Honey ranges in color from light to dark, the paler stuff typically being milder tasting. To avoid crystallization, stored it in an airtight container at room temperature. When measuring honey, spray a glass measuring cup with a bit of nonstick spray so it will pour out easily.

Maple-Glazed Parsnips and Carrots

QuickEase

*Orange and white are the color of the day, flecked with slivers
of green. A maple-citrus glaze complements both the
nuttiness of parsnips and the sweetness of carrots.*

Serves 8
5 parsnips, thickly sliced
5 carrots, thickly sliced
1/4 cup orange juice
1 tablespoon maple syrup
1 teaspoon butter, melted
1/2 teaspoon dried dill
1/4 teaspoon salt

1. Combine all the ingredients in the slow cooker.
2. Cook on LOW for 8 to 10 hours, or on HIGH for 4 to
   5 hours.

Tip: Parsnips are a root vegetable shaped like carrots
but creamy white in color. They taste slightly sweet and
are popular in soups and stews. When buying parsnips,
avoid larger ones, because they often have an inedible
woody core. Choose firm, unspotted parsnips, and store
in the fridge.

String Beans Italiano

WhamBam

String beans, or green beans as they are often called, are smothered in Italian tomato sauce and ready to share plate-space with any entrée.

Serves 4

1 pound string beans
1 (14-ounce) can tomato sauce
1 tablespoon Italian seasoning

1. Place the string beans in the slow cooker.
2. In a bowl, mix together the sauce and Italian seasoning, and pour over the beans.
3. Cook on LOW for 6 to 8 hours, or on HIGH for 3 to 4 hours.

Tip: Tomato sauce is available preseasoned with different herb blends, so go ahead and use your favorite and omit the Italian seasoning.

Color My World Indeed

I'm never helping my husband with a home renovation project again. Last weekend, we decided to paint the kitchen, but by the time I'd picked out a nice painting outfit, Hubby was rolling away. So he stuck me with the painstaking job of doing the trim. Naturally, I was still on my first foot of baseboard when Mr. Competitive finished all the walls! At this point, my hand was getting sore so I decided to take a break. He started ragging on me 'cause I didn't clean my brush. *Holy dictator!* I thought. *Do I have to do everything?* Then I got a great idea and put the brush in the dishwasher. Dripping sarcasm, he asked if I'd checked the handle to see if it was dishwasher safe. So I said something snippy to him and he said something snippy to me, but just as the fireworks started to fly, an old saying occurred to me: If you can't take the heat, get out of the kitchen. So I did.

V3 Parisienne

QuickEase

Lovely little balls of zucchini, tomatoes, and potatoes baked in a buttery basil blend. Ah, the wonders of a melon baller.

Serves 6
2 zucchini
2 pounds Parisienne-style potatoes
1 pint cherry tomatoes
2 tablespoons butter, melted
1 tablespoon olive oil
2 teaspoons dried basil
1/4 teaspoon salt
1/4 teaspoon pepper

1. Using a melon baller, scoop out zucchini into little balls, and place in slow cooker along with the potatoes and tomatoes.
2. In a bowl, mix together the butter, olive oil, basil, salt, and pepper, and pour over the vegetables, stirring to ensure all the vegetables are coated.
3. Cook on LOW for 6 to 8 hours, or on HIGH for 3 to 4 hours.

 Tip: A melon baller is a handy, inexpensive gadget available in the kitchen accessories section of most department stores and supermarkets.

Zucchini Parmigiana

QuickEase

*Layer after layer of thick zucchini slices, spicy tomato sauce,
and creamy ricotta and mozzarella cheeses, topped off
with a generous dusting of Parmesan.*

Serves 6
1 cup tomato sauce
1 teaspoon Italian seasoning
$1/2$ cup ricotta cheese
$1/2$ cup grated mozzarella cheese
3 zucchini, thickly sliced
3 tablespoons grated Parmesan cheese

1. Combine the tomato sauce and Italian seasoning, and cover the bottom of the slow cooker with a thin layer of the mixture.
2. Mix together the ricotta and mozzarella cheese.
3. Place a layer of zucchini, followed by a layer of the cheese mixture in the slow cooker, and repeat.
4. Pour the remaining sauce over the top, and sprinkle with Parmesan.
5. Cook on LOW for 2 to 3 hours.

 Tip: If you like eggplant, use it instead of zucchini or try a combination.

Sugar Squash

WhamBam

The perfect accompaniment to ham or pork on a crisp autumn day.
So easy you will have plenty of time to frolic, guilt-free.

Serves 4

2 acorn *or* butternut squashes
2 teaspoons butter
4 tablespoons maple syrup

1. Halve the squashes crosswise and remove the pulp.
2. Place 1/2 teaspoon of butter and 1 tablespoon of maple syrup into the cavity of each squash half.
3. Transfer the squash to the slow cooker, stacking if necessary.
4. Cook on LOW for 8 to 10 hours, or on HIGH for 4 to 5 hours.

Tip: Real maple syrup tastes best, but the artificial stuff will do.

The Guilty Party

That's it. I'm not going to any more home parties where you're guilt-tripped into purchasing some product you don't like. Oh sure, your friend assures you there'll be no pressure. And, it's all nicey-nicey at the beginning. Have some paté, Rebecca; I love your hair. But then, Head Honcho Woman takes over. After thanking everyone for coming, she drops the bomb that the charming hostess won't get a free gift unless you all drop a wad of dough. So, you glance at your friend, praying she'll be rolling her eyes, but no, her baby blues are big fat saucers overflowing with greed. Are you going to be the one to deprive her? What if people think you're cheap? Omigod, what if they think you're having *financial problems*? So you buy whatever, come home, and put up with Hubby calling you a sucker all night. The worst part? Knowing he's right.

Trees and Cheese

WhamBam

Wickedly easy, here broccoli and cauliflower "trees"
are slow cooked in a buttery cheese sauce.

Serves 6

1 (16 ounce) package frozen broccoli
   and cauliflower mix
1 (10-ounce) can condensed Cheddar
   cheese soup
1 tablespoon butter

1. Combine the broccoli and cauliflower
   and Cheddar cheese soup in the slow
   cooker.
2. Place the butter on top.
3. Cook on **LOW** for 3 to 4 hours, stir,
   and serve.

Tip: As this dish cooks, the moisture from the veggies provides
enough liquid to ensure the sauce
doesn't get too thick, so there's no
need to dilute the soup.

Sign in Ladies' Change Room at the Gym

To Our Valued Members . . .

- We are glad you love your body. But
  not everyone does, so please, throw
  on a towel or something more than a
  curling iron while your fixing your hair.
- We are glad you love your voice. But
  not everyone does, so please, wait to
  tell your workout buddy about your
  recent trip to the gynecologist once
  you're both out of the shower.
- We are glad you love your stuff. But
  not everyone does, so please, try to
  keep your water bottle, towel, tooth-
  brush, toothpaste, comb, gel, bar-
  rettes, elastics, deodorant, lotion,
  powder, body wash, facial wipes,
  toner, moisturizer, foundation, blush,
  eye shadow, mascara, lipstick, panties,
  bra, tights, camisole, blouse, blazer,
  skirt, boots, coat, purse, cell phone,
  portable CD-player, briefcase, watch,
  necklace, bracelet, earrings, and belly-
  button ring in the little half locker
  you've been allocated. *Or bring less.*

Red-Hot Ladies' Fingers

WhamBam

A simple version of a Louisiana favorite featuring okra pods, otherwise known as ladies' fingers, bathed in a spicy tomato sauce.

Serves 4

1 pound okra, washed, tips removed
1 (28-ounce) can plum tomatoes
1/4 teaspoon cayenne

1. Combine all the ingredients in the slow cooker.
2. Cook on LOW for 4 to 6 hours, or on HIGH for 2 to 3 hours.

 Tip: When purchasing okra, select crisp, bright green pods.

Voodoo Magic

If you want to keep your man faithful, give Voodoo a try. All you need is a doll, a personal item belonging to your mate, and a big pin. Technically, you're supposed to make the doll out of moss and twigs, but you can omit the crafty part, and use your daughter's Ken doll instead.

Step 1: When your man is not alert (big window of time here), cut off some of his hair.

Step 2: Tape it to Ken's head.

Step 3: Make Ken anatomically correct by cutting an eraser snub off the end of a pencil and gluing it you know where.

Step 4: This is the fun part. Take a long black pin and slowly stick it into Ken's privates.
(This is not the fun part for Ken.)

Step 5: Hide Ken.

Step 6: Replace Ken doll so your daughter won't grow up with your fear that men will vanish.

Apple and Apricot Chutney

QuickEase

*Sweet, sticky, and absolutely delicious, this makes a perfect
"cooldown" alongside a spicy meal, or with grilled meat.*

Yields 3¹/2 cups
4 tart cooking apples, peeled, cubed
1 small onion, chopped
1 clove garlic, minced
1 cup chopped dried apricots
¹/2 cup brown sugar
¹/4 cup apple juice
¹/3 cup white wine vinegar
2 pieces crystallized ginger, chopped
1 cinnamon stick
¹/8 teaspoon dried thyme

1. Combine all the ingredients in the slow cooker.
2. Cook on HIGH for 1 hour.
3. Place the lid askew and continue cooking for an additional
   1¹/2 to 2 hours on HIGH, or until most of the liquid is
   evaporated.
4. Remove and discard the cinnamon stick; serve warm,
   chilled, or at room temperature.

 Tip: Next time you're invited to a barbecue, bring this
dish along in a pretty glass jar.

Homemade Baby Food

33 Minutes

If you really get into making love and dinner at the same time, ultimately, you may end up with an extra little person at the table. There is no easier way to make nutritious, homemade baby food than in your slow cooker.

2 cups

Fruits

5 or 6 whole fruits, peeled and sliced (pears, peaches, apples, etc.)
2 or 3 teaspoons water

1. Place the fruit and water in the slow cooker.
2. Cook on LOW for 4 to 6 hours, or until the fruit is tender.
3. Transfer to a blender or food processor, and purée until smooth.

Vegetables

2½ cups vegetables, peeled, sliced (carrots, potatoes, squash, string beans, etc.)
Water to cover

1. Place the vegetables and water in the slow cooker.
2. Cook on LOW for 4 to 8 hours, or until the vegetables are tender.
3. Drain, reserving liquid, and transfer to blender or food processor; purée until smooth, adding a bit of reserved liquid as needed.

 Tip: For ease and convenience, freeze baby food in ice-cube containers; then transfer to freezer bags so you can take cubes out as needed.

The Afterglow—
Beverages and Desserts

recipe list continued on following page

There's a fine line between Crock-Pot® and crackpot, and if you find yourself trying to bake a pie in your slow cooker, you've taken a giant step across it. Darling, go to a bakery, or feed the family a brick of ice cream. Pastries and flaky things don't lend themselves well to slow cooking, and even if they did, few women know how to knead (that's knead with a *k*, people), and most lack the time for such creations.

Which doesn't mean homemade desserts are out of your repertoire entirely. On the contrary, fabulous desserts such as bread puddings, pudding cakes, custards, and stewed fruit are ideal in the slow cooker. Unlike pastries, such dishes benefit from long cooking times, steady low temperatures, and a moist environment in which natural or processed sugars won't scorch. And, they're sinfully easy to make. Throw in a few sliced plums, sugar, and a bit of liqueur, and suddenly you've got a delightful after-dinner treat that begs for whipped cream. And let's face it, anything that begs for whipped cream can't be all bad. Many an evening has turned happily erotic by simply placing a can on the table and asking Hubby if he'd like to squirt.

And many an evening has turned happily erotic with just the right amount of spirits. So, in addition to a few nonalcoholic beverages, I've included some that are spiked. On a cold night, both types will make you hot. Too much of the latter will make you think you're hot, anyway. Do keep in mind that sugar, spices, and other ingredients often mask the taste of alcohol in a heated drink, so if you decide to down multiple mugs of Hot Lemon Remedy or The Slurring Earl it's entirely possible you'll end up peeling off your long underwear and mooning the moon from the balcony. In any case, these pots of pleasure are perfect for entertaining, or after a playful day on the slopes. And yes, escalators in malls count as slopes.

In today's world of fat-bashing, fitness, and feng shui, many people opt to deprive themselves of dessert altogether. Me, I like to fit it in now and then and worry about fitting into my clothes later. After all, I rationalize, the only thing worse than too much of a bad thing is too little of a good one. And eating dessert *is* good. In a way, it's like sex—for best results, just close your eyes, try not to think too much, and enjoy it while it lasts.

Vienna Coffee

33 Minutes

A nonalcoholic, specialty coffee perfect after dinner,
or any time you feel like a pick-me-up treat.

Serves 4
6 cups strong hot coffee
1/4 cup sugar (optional)
5 whole cloves
4 whole allspice berries
3 cinnamon sticks, broken
Whipped cream

1. Combine the brewed coffee and sugar in the slow cooker.
2. Place cloves, allspice, and cinnamon sticks on a small square of cheesecloth, form into a sack, tie with kitchen string, and drop into slow cooker.
3. Cook on LOW for 3 to 4 hours.
4. Remove and discard the cheesecloth sack, and serve in heatproof glasses with a dollop of whipped cream.

 Tip: Sprinkle with nutmeg or cinnamon if desired.

The Slurring Earl

QuickEase

It's teatime like no other. The ladies will love this hot and tangy pot of goodness. Caution: Just because you can't taste the vodka, doesn't mean it's not there.

Serves 6
4 Earl Grey tea bags
¼ cup dried cranberries
2 cups boiling water
4 cups cranberry cocktail
¼ cup honey
1 cup vodka

1. Place the tea bags and dried cranberries in the slow cooker, add the boiling water, and let steep for 5 minutes.
2. Remove and discard the tea bags, and add the cranberry cocktail and honey.
3. Cook on HIGH for 2 hours.
4. Add the vodka, and serve immediately.

 Tip: Keep the slow cooker on LOW or WARM setting so guests can help themselves right out of the slow cooker.

Hot Lemon Remedy

QuickEase

A comforting, hot lemony drink certain to wash away your worries.

Serves 4
4 lemon tea bags
2 cups boiling water
¼ cup honey
1 cinnamon stick
2 whole cloves
1 bottle dry white wine

1. Combine the tea bags and boiling water in the slow cooker; let steep for 10 minutes, and remove and discard tea bags.
2. Stir in the honey, cinnamon stick, cloves, and wine.
3. Cook on **LOW** for 2 to 3 hours; remove and discard the cinnamon stick and cloves, and serve.

Tip: Add a few slices of lemon for garnish.

Telephone Etiquette Hotline

Yes, um, I have a question about caller ID. Just because everyone has it now, does that mean, as a society, we no longer have to leave messages? Personally, I get very upset when the amount of new numbers on my ID list doesn't equal the amount of messages I received. I worry my voice mail's not working, or someone called who's dying, or a caller assumes I'll call them back because they know I know they called. So to be safe, I call every number on my list. But people can't remember why they called, or deny they called me (which is ridiculous, I tell them, because I have proof), or some even ask me if I have nothing better to do. Most humiliating is calling numbers I don't recognize. I tell them I'm calling to find out why they were calling and they tell me to stop calling or they'll call the police! Anyway, I desperately need answers, so call me back immediately. And if I'm not home, *please leave a message*.

Mulled Wine

QuickEase

Red wine marries well with spices. This is the surest way to thaw even the chilliest heart.

Serves 6
2 bottles dry red wine
1 cup water
1/2 cup sugar
Juice of 1 orange
4 cloves, whole
4 allspice, whole
2 cinnamon sticks, broken

1. Combine the wine, water, sugar, and juice in the slow cooker.
2. Place the cloves, allspice, and cinnamon sticks on a small square of cheesecloth, form into a sack, tie with kitchen string, and drop into wine mixture.
3. Cook on HIGH for 2 hours; remove the cheesecloth sack, and serve.

 Tip: Keep wine warm in the slow cooker on **LOW** or **WARM** setting.

Wedding Party Rules

It's an honor to be in a friend's wedding party, but such a stressful event. Maybe there should be a few rules so that everyone, not only the bride, has a special day.

1. If any woman in the wedding party has ever breastfed, backless dresses are out. So, too, are skintight gowns, if any woman is more than 4 pounds overweight.
2. If any woman in the wedding party has no cheekbones, poofy hairdos are out. Bad enough one must go through life looking like a chipmunk, let's not plant a wooly mammoth on her head.
3. If any woman in the wedding party isn't a millionaire, buying a present for every shower she attends is out. The woman has already agreed to pay for a dress, shoes, and accessories that she'll never again be caught dead in—consider that a gift.

Wassail

QuickEase

A hot fruity wine punch guests can help
themselves to right out of the crock.

Serves 6
1 bottle red wine
3 cups apple cider
2 tablespoons orange peel
4 whole cloves
2 cinnamon sticks, broken
1 piece crystallized ginger

1. Pour the wine and cider into the slow cooker.
2. Place the orange peel, cloves, cinnamon sticks, and ginger on a small square of cheesecloth, form into a sack, tie with kitchen string, and drop into wine mixture.
3. Cook on LOW for 2 hours; remove the cheesecloth sack, and serve.

 Tip: If you prefer a nonalcoholic punch, omit the red wine and use an additional 3 cups of apple cider.

Peachy Keen

QuickEase

A supersweet treat the kids will love. Spike your own mug with a shot of amber rum if you're in the mood.

Serves 6

1 cup peach crystals
1/4 cup brown sugar
2 pieces crystallized ginger, diced
8 cups water

1. Combine all the ingredients in the slow cooker.
2. Cook on LOW for 4 or 6 hours.

 Tip: To jazz this beverage up a bit, add a few pieces of dried fruit such as apple rings or peach slices—the fruit will plump up during the long cooking time.

Half the Fun Is Getting There!

I'm so excited. Tomorrow, we're going on our family vacation. I'm glad we decided to drive—why pay all that money to fly when we can spend 7 or 8 or 9 or so hours of quality time together in the car? My husband knows how to get there. Of course, just in case, I'll have my trusty map and I'll make suggestions and Hubby will squeeze my hand and thank me for my uncanny sense of direction. The kids will nestle contentedly in the backseat, doing the I-Love-Math workbooks I bought them, and sharing their 1 electronic toy. And everyone will love the lunch I've packed—I bet those bananas will be the first to go! Yes, everything's going to be so peachy keen, when we arrive, we'll probably be sorry the trip is over! Oh well, at least we can look forward to the long drive home.

Hot Choc Butterscotch Crock

QuickEase

A delicious combination of hot chocolate and butterscotch
schnapps sure to slide down your throat like liquid candy.

Serves 4

3 cups dry skim milk powder

1/2 cup unsweetened cocoa powder

1/2 cup sugar

6 cups water

1 teaspoon vanilla extract

1 cup butterscotch *or* butter ripple schnapps

1. Combine the skim milk powder, cocoa powder, and sugar in the slow cooker.
2. Whisk in the water and vanilla, stirring until smooth.
3. Cook on **LOW** for 4 to 5 hours.
4. Stir in the schnapps, and serve.

Tip: If the kids are around, serve them the hot chocolate first, put them to bed, and then add the schnapps for you and Hubby.

Hot Buttered Rum

*Amber or dark rum is lovely heated amidst butter, cinnamon,
nutmeg, and cloves. Rum quantity may be adjusted
up or down, depending on the crowd.*

Serves 4
1 1/2 cups brown sugar
1/4 cup butter
1/2 teaspoon ground nutmeg
1/2 teaspoon ground cinnamon
1/4 teaspoon ground cloves
5 cups water
1 1/2 cups amber *or* dark rum

1. Combine all the ingredients *except* the rum in the slow
   cooker.
2. Cook on LOW for 4 to 6 hours.
3. Add rum just before serving.

 Tip: To make this dish more punchlike, add a 14-ounce
can of pineapple tidbits with juices.

Group Hugs

WhamBam

Dried cranberries and whole roasted almonds snuggled in elegant white chocolate. So pretty they make the perfect gift; so good, they're hard to part with.

Makes 10
6 squares white chocolate
1/3 cup whole roasted almonds
1/3 cup dried cranberries

1. Place the chocolate in a single layer on the bottom of the slow cooker, and sprinkle the almonds and cranberries on top.
2. Cook on LOW for 1 1/2 to 2 hours, or until the chocolate is soft but not completely melted.
3. Turn off the slow cooker, stir the ingredients well, and drop by spoonfuls onto a tray lined with wax paper.
4. Chill for a few hours before serving.

 Tips: These make a lovely gift simply wrapped in cellophane and tied with a bow.

Hugger's Help Line

Could someone please tell me the rules on hugging? Everyone's doing it these days and I need to know whom I'm supposed to hug, when I'm supposed to hug them, how hard, and for how long. For instance, when I meet someone I know quite well, a hug seems clearly in order. But if I run into a neighbor at the supermarket and I may have lent her my chainsaw once, are we mere strangers supposed to embrace? Or when I'm leaving a friend's house, is it necessary for us to hug goodbye? If I were going to sail around the world I would be so inclined, but it seems dramatic when I'm just going to walk around the corner. The problem is compounded if her husband is there—am I required to wrap my arms around him, too? If so, does the hug-fest end with the children? Or extend to the family cat? Please advise.

Pineapple Rice Pudding

QuickEase

Delightful bits of pineapple add a refreshing zip to this comfort-food classic. Creamy, rich, and easy to make especially if you've got leftover rice on hand.

Serves 4

2 cups cooked rice

1/4 cup diced dried pineapple

1 (13-ounce) can evaporated milk

2 tablespoons butter, melted

2 tablespoons sugar

1 teaspoon vanilla extract

1. Combine the rice and pineapple in the slow cooker.
2. In a bowl, mix together the remaining ingredients, and pour into slow cooker.
3. Cook on HIGH for 2½ to 3 hours.

 Tip: For traditional rice pudding, use raisins instead of pineapple and sprinkle a bit of cinnamon over the top.

Hugger's Help Line: Part 2

Hello, it's me again, with a few more inquiries about hugging. As I said, a hugging craze is sweeping the nation, and I want very much to get it right. Okay, I need to know who ends the hug. Is it rude to be the first to break it off, or viewed as needy to keep hanging on? And how much muscle power do I put into it? Are the huggee's feet supposed to leave the ground, or am I supposed to just squeeze and pat the back? If I hug too hard, will I become known as a hugging machine? Or, if I hug too gently, will I be labeled a lackadaisical hugger? Which is worse? Anyway, please provide information immediately. I am attending a social function tonight, and don't want people talking about me behind my back.

Custard Caramel

33 Minutes

Spoon-feed this dessert into his mouth and you'll be able to sweet-talk any man into anything. Lovely, lovely stuff.

Serves 6

3/4 cup plus 3 tablespoons sugar

1/4 cup water

3 eggs

2 cups milk

3 tablespoons cream

1 tablespoon vanilla

1. In a saucepan, combine the 3/4 cup sugar and the water over medium-high heat. Stir constantly until the sugar is dissolved and the mixture comes to a boil.
2. Stop stirring and let the mixture cook for 4 minutes or until the mixture turns golden brown.
3. Pour the mixture into a 6-cup round baking dish that has been sprayed with nonstick spray, distributing the mixture evenly along the bottom and up the sides a bit.
4. In a bowl, beat the eggs and the remaining sugar until lemony yellow; stir in the milk, cream, and vanilla; and pour the mixture into the baking dish.
5. Cover tightly with foil and secure with an elastic band; transfer to slow cooker, and pour enough water into the slow cooker so that it comes up 1 inch on the sides of baking dish.
6. Cook on HIGH for 4 hours or until a toothpick inserted in the center comes out clean.
7. Chill for at least 4 hours, and serve.

 Tip: To remove the custard, run a knife along the edges to pry it from the sides.

Brown Sugar Fruit Sundaes

QuickEase

*Apples, nectarines, raisins, and plums stewed in a cider and
brown sugar syrup, chilled, and then nestled between
layers of vanilla ice cream. In a word, awesome.*

Yields 4 cups
3 plums, unpeeled
3 nectarines, unpeeled
2 apples, unpeeled
1/3 cup raisins
1/2 cup brown sugar
1/4 teaspoon ground cinnamon
1/4 cup apple cider
1 quart vanilla ice cream

1. Slice the fruits over the slow cooker so the slices and juices
   drop into it.
2. Stir in the raisins, brown sugar, cinnamon, and cider.
3. Cook on LOW for 3 to 4 hours.
4. Serve chilled, layered between ice cream in 8- to 10-ounce
   glasses or sundae dishes. To create sundaes, place 1/4 cup of
   ice cream in the bottom of each glass. Add 1/4 cup fruit
   mixture, another 1/4 cup ice cream, and top with an
   additional 1/4 cup fruit.

 Tip: While other fruits can be used, this recipe saves
time by calling for types you don't have to peel.

Plums in Brandy Soak

QuickEase

4 plums, 2 people, a couple of shots of brandy, and 1 can of whipped cream. 'Tis the makings of a spirited evening, no?

Serves 2

4 ripe plums, unpeeled
¼ cup boiling water
¼ cup sugar
¼ cup brandy
Whipped cream

1. Halve and pit the plums, and place in slow cooker.
2. Mix together the boiling water and sugar, and pour over the plums.
3. Cook on LOW for 3 hours, and stir in brandy.
4. Stir in the brandy, and cook for an additional 30 minutes on LOW; serve with whipped cream.

 Tip: Choose ripe, sweet plums for this dessert; if sour, you'll require more sugar.

How to Pick Up a Man in a Supermarket: Part 3

Welcome, ladies, to the final part of our class. We begin here in whipped cream. Grab a can, pop the lid, and spray. Now, yelp with surprise as gobs of creamy white stuff go flying! Lovely! Okay, on to frozen foods. The trick here is to look cool, but not frigid. Lean over a freezer, and suck up that cold Arctic air. Now, to maintain your newfound perky state, set a brick of ice cream in the top part of your cart, rest your breasts on top, and run to the checkout! Look, there's a man chasing you! Congratu—oh dear, you grabbed the wrong cart? Well, gush or something! Dear heavens, what are you doing? You can't *literally* pick a man up and throw him in your cart! It's not in the lesson plan! Oh, all right, wheel him out before he regains consciousness! Go! Go! Go!

Stewed Green Apples

QuickEase

*A fabulous dessert of apples stewed in a buttery sweet syrup so easy to make,
practically anyone can do it. Older kids, say, or Hubby . . .*

Serves 4

4 Granny Smith apples,
   peeled, thinly sliced
2 tablespoons butter,
   melted
2 tablespoons sugar
1/4 teaspoon cinnamon

1. Combine all the ingredients
in the slow cooker.
2. Cook on LOW for 3 or
4 hours.

 Tip: If you would like,
try a few chopped nuts
on top.

A Mother's Day Wish

This year for Mother's Day, wouldn't it be nice if Hubby and
the kids did the little things around the house it seems only
we mothers do? You know, stuff like:

- Place a fresh toilet paper roll in its dispenser instead of
leaving it on the bathroom counter.
- Empty the garbage bag under the sink BEFORE it
overflows.
- Make a pitcher of juice from frozen concentrate even
though swirling the icy cylinder around until it melts
seems like a lot of work.
- Put away folded laundry instead of rummaging through
the basket and leaving it rumpled to magically fold again.
- Hang something. Maybe not wallpaper, but a towel, say,
or a coat.
- Close something. The front door, a kitchen cupboard, a
box of cereal.
- Turn something off. The TV in the living room. The TV
in the family room. The TV upstairs.
- Find something. A lid to a plastic sandwich container,
my sewing scissors, a roll of any kind of tape.
- Give something water. A houseplant, the hamster, an
empty ice-cube tray.
- Say something. Anything really, but how about something
nice like: *Gee, your hair smells terrific* . . . or *No, no, no,
I'll do it* . . . or *Hey, let's make every day Mother's Day!*

Walnut-Coated Apples with Cinnamon Stick Pierce

QuickEase

Apples, stuffed with raisins, rolled in walnuts, sprinkled with brown sugar, then pierced with a stick of cinnamon. Delicious.

Serves 4

4 apples	⅓ cup walnut pieces,	¼ cup raisins
¼ cup butter,	slightly crushed	4 teaspoons brown
melted	4 cinnamon sticks, whole	sugar

1. Core the apples using an apple corer that removes the core but doesn't slice the apple into sections. Turn each apple on its side and push the corer through the apple, creating a hole on each side.
2. Peel the top half of each apple, and dip the peeled end into the butter, and then into the walnut crumbs.
3. "Pierce" the apple with a cinnamon stick by running it through the holes on each side.
4. Mix the raisins with 2 teaspoons of the brown sugar.
5. Holding the cinnamon stick so it is centered, stuff the raisin mixture into the top and bottom holes of the apple, adding enough stuffing so that the cinnamon stick is secure.
6. Transfer the apples to the slow cooker, and sprinkle with the remaining brown sugar and butter.
7. Cook on LOW for 2 to 3 hours or until the apples are tender.

 Tip: It is best to eat these sticky treats with a knife and fork.

Shivering Candy Cane Pears

QuickEase

A taste of Christmas as cold and refreshing as a breath of winter air. Candy canes cause the pears to blush a pretty pink amidst their sweet, minty syrup.

Serves 4

2 (6-inch) candy canes, broken into pieces,
  or 6 red-and-white-striped candy mints
1½ cups boiling water
½ cup sugar
4 Anjou pears, peeled, halved

1. Place the candy cane pieces and boiling water in the slow cooker and let stand for 15 minutes.
2. Stir in the sugar until dissolved; then stir in the pears.
3. Cook on LOW for 3 to 4 hours.
4. Chill, and serve.

 Tip: Anjou pears are shaped like eggs, and have pale green, yellowish, or reddish skin. Because they are sweet as well as juicy, they're fabulous poached and served as dessert.

The Way the Cookie Grumbles

It's about cookie exchanges. You know, those preholiday parties where everyone brings so many dozen of 1 type of cookie, exchanges them with everyone else, and leaves with the same amount of cookies, only different types. It sounds good in theory. But the trouble is, there's a huge discrepancy in people's cookie standards. Like, if I spend next month's mortgage on real butter for melt-in-your-mouth shortbreads, I don't want to bring home crappy, store-bought sugar-infested delights. And what's with the peanut butter balls? Are they even Christmasy? And please, somebody make decorating mandatory. C'mon folks, it's the holidays, so give a little. Last year I got a dozen plain gingerbread men that looked like little naked boys staring blindly from the plate!

Drunken Orange Rings

33 Minutes

A delightfully syrupy dessert of orange rings, soaked in liqueur, chilled, and served straight up, or over ice cream.

Serves 4

5 oranges	1 cup sugar
1 cup water	2 tablespoons orange liqueur

1. Remove the zest from 1 orange and place the zest in a small saucepan along with the water; cook for 5 minutes over medium-high heat.
2. Meanwhile, with a sharp knife, remove the skin and white pith from the oranges.
3. Slice the oranges crosswise into rings, and place them in the slow cooker.
4. Using a small strainer, carefully remove the zest from the liquid in the saucepan, and discard the zest.
5. Stir the sugar into the liquid, bring to a boil, and let cook for 5 minutes or until the liquid thickens into a syrup.
6. Remove from heat, stir in the orange liqueur, and pour the mixture over the orange rings in the slow cooker.
7. Cook on LOW for 2 to 3 hours.
8. Chill, and serve.

 Tip: This is an ideal make-ahead dessert that you can cook the evening before, and then chill until ready to serve.

Sweet Peach Crisp

QuickEase

*A fabulous way to end a meal. Canned peaches, cinnamon,
and brown sugar become warm and wonderful
beneath a crispy granola topping.*

Serves 4
1 (28-ounce) can sliced peaches
$^1/_2$ cup brown sugar
$^1/_3$ cup flour
2 teaspoons lemon juice
$^1/_2$ teaspoon cinnamon
$^2/_3$ cup granola

1. Spray the slow cooker with nonstick spray.
2. Drain the peaches, reserving juice for another use.
3. Combine the drained peaches, brown sugar, flour, lemon
   juice, cinnamon, and $^1/_3$ cup of the granola in the slow
   cooker.
4. Sprinkle the remaining granola on top.
5. Cook on LOW for 4 to 6 hours.

 Tip: Canned peaches are typically the clingstone variety
with flesh that clings to the pit, as its name implies.
This dessert is lovely as is, but to-die-for served with ice
cream and a handful of your favorite fresh berries.

Bananas in Warm Honey-Ginger Syrup

QuickEase

Go bananas over ice cream with this tropically inspired, decadent dessert oozing with sweetness and a kiss of ginger.

Serves 4

4 ripe bananas, sliced lengthwise
    and halved
²/₃ cup orange juice
1 tablespoon honey
1 piece crystallized ginger, chopped
2 teaspoons shredded unsweetened
    coconut
¹/₂ teaspoon ground cinnamon

1. Combine all the ingredients in the slow cooker.
2. Cook on **LOW** for 3 to 4 hours.

 Tip: Serve over ice cream, and sprinkle with brown sugar and nuts, if desired.

What's Not in the Vacation Guide

Ah, the Caribbean. An all-inclusive week for 2 during which you and your man will do nothing but make love, talk, and spend time together, right? *Well.* In addition to food and beverages, tropical holidays include other things:

- **Lots of women.** Try to remember while your man's eyeballs are ricocheting around in their sockets like marbles in a pinball machine, ultimately, he only has eyes for you.
- **Lots of men.** Try to remember while your man is busy bonding with every beer-swilling bozo he head-butts, ultimately, his strongest connection is with you.
- **Lots of activities.** Try to remember while your man is off winning deep-sea fishing and extreme dolphin-riding championships, ultimately, his greatest prize is you.
- **Lots of ocean.** Try to remember to remind him that there are lots of other fish in the sea.

Apple Pie Pudding Melt

QuickEase

An easy-to-make family favorite, guaranteed to please.

Serves 4
6 cups cubed stale bread
4 apples, peeled, chopped
3/4 cup apple juice
1/4 cup pineapple juice
1/4 cup brown sugar
1/2 teaspoon cinnamon
1/4 teaspoon nutmeg
1/8 teaspoon cloves

1. Spray the slow cooker with nonstick spray.
2. Combine the bread and apples in the slow cooker.
3. In a small bowl, combine the apple juice, pineapple juice, brown sugar, cinnamon, nutmeg, and cloves; pour into the slow cooker and stir to combine.
4. Cook on LOW for 5 to 6 hours.

 Tip: This recipe fits nicely in a small slow cooker, but if you have a larger one, go ahead and double it. You can use 1 teaspoon of apple pie spice instead of the cinnamon, nutmeg, and cloves.

Are You Ready for Baby?

Introducing RoboBaby, the first robotic baby designed to test a woman's readiness for motherhood. Our month-long program simulates the newborn experience, beginning with a huge financial investment that will completely deplete a couple's resources. To simulate childbirth, our team of professionals will come to your home and, without anesthetic, extract 1 of your teeth. (Please note: Daddy-to-be will get all the sympathy because he has to watch.) From then on, all hell breaks loose as RoboBaby cries incessantly, demands feeding day and night, and releases exploding stink pellets willy-nilly. Our sophisticated monitoring system enables us to track your responses, as RoboBaby sends out electronic signals every time it is picked up, changed, or fed! Upon program completion, you'll receive a detailed analysis of your efforts. Please note, regardless of failure or success, there are no returns or refunds—and, there are certainly no guarantees.

Chocolate-Orange Bread Pudding

33 Minutes

A happy ending to a family meal, sure to sweeten everyone's mood. Bread puddings are a natural for slow cookers, and ideal for the baking-impaired.

Serves 4

6 cups cubed stale bread
3 cups milk
1½ cups sugar
1 cup unsweetened cocoa powder
2 eggs
1 tablespoon vanilla extract
2 tablespoons marmalade

1. Spray the inside of the slow cooker with nonstick spray.
2. Place the bread in the slow cooker.
3. In a saucepan, combine the milk, sugar, and cocoa powder; cook over medium-high heat for 4 minutes, whisking constantly.
4. Whisk in the eggs and vanilla, remove from heat, and stir in the marmalade; pour the mixture over the bread in the slow cooker, making sure all the pieces are covered.
5. Cook on HIGH for 4 hours.

 Tip: If you'd like to make a more adult-friendly bread pudding, omit marmalade and use 2 or 3 tablespoons of Irish cream liqueur instead.

Crispy Rice Cereal Nests

WhamBam

The kids will love these edible nests that are ideal for holding candy worms, jellybeans, chocolate eggs, or any other type of candy. A terrific birthday party treat!

Makes 12
1 (8-ounce) bag mini-marshmallows
¼ cup butter, melted
6 cups crispy rice cereal

1. Spray the inside of the slow cooker with nonstick spray.
2. Combine the marshmallows and butter in the slow cooker.
3. Cook on LOW for 1 to 1½ hours.
4. Stir in the crispy rice cereal.
5. Spray a muffin tin pan with nonstick spray, and using a large spoon, drop spoonfuls of the mixture into the muffin tin, filling until level.
6. Using the back of a greased tablespoon, press into the center of each to create little nests, and let cool.

 Tip: This recipe is a good way to introduce older children to the slow cooker, as it's a safe and easy way to make a kid's favorite!

Planning a Child's Birthday Party 101

Gone are the days when balloons are enough; today's bashes are elaborate affairs that can make or break a kid's popularity.

- THE LOOT BAG—No penny candy—too Halloweeny. No dollar store crap—too cheap. And nothing practical, unless you want your kid to be known as the Nerd Who Gave Out Rulers. Think expensive. Think electronics.
- THE THEME—Forget generic decorations, get the superhero of the day. And not just hats—a real-live action character. Think costume rental. Think Hubby in tights.
- THE PLACE—Pick a spot that is original, but not different. Avoid anywhere educational—if it even feels like a field trip, your kid's social life is history. Think big. Think Disney.

Banana-Cinnamon-Coconut Bread

QuickEase

Cinnamon and coconut gently push classic banana bread into the new millennium. Fabulous with morning coffee and someone special.

1 loaf

1³/₄ cups flour	¹/₃ cup shortening
1 teaspoon baking powder	2 eggs
¹/₂ teaspoon ground cinnamon	2 ripe bananas, mashed
¹/₂ teaspoon salt	1 tablespoon shredded,
¹/₂ cup sugar	unsweetened coconut

1. In a bowl, sift together the flour, baking powder, cinnamon, and salt.
2. In another bowl, combine the sugar and shortening, and add the eggs.
3. Beat the mixture until fluffy, add the bananas, and mix well.
4. Add the coconut and dry ingredients, and blend quickly.
5. Spray a loaf tin with nonstick spray, and pour the mixture into the tin.
6. Cover tightly with foil, and transfer tin to the slow cooker.
7. Cook on HIGH, checking for doneness after 2 hours.

 Tip: Before beginning this recipe, check to make sure you have a loaf tin that fits inside your slow cooker. For tomorrow morning's snack, cook the evening before, let cool, and wrap tightly in foil.

Fruit-and-Nut Roll

QuickEase

*Raisins, walnuts, pecans, almonds, and honey cuddle up in a rich, buttery
pastry roll. Good served with coffee. Great served with coffee in bed.*

Serves 4

1/2 cup butter

1 1/2 cups flour

1/4 cup sugar

2 egg yolks

1/8 teaspoon salt

1/8 teaspoon cinnamon

3 tablespoons cold water

1/4 cup honey

1/4 cup raisins

1/3 cup chopped almonds

1/3 cup chopped pecans

1/3 cup chopped walnuts

1. In a bowl, cut the butter into the flour using a pastry cutter or 2 knives;
   then stir in sugar.
2. Create well in the center, add the egg yolks, and stir to form a paste.
3. Stir in the salt, cinnamon, and water, and form into a ball.
4. Cover in plastic wrap and refrigerate for at least 2 hours or overnight.
5. On a floured work surface, roll out the refrigerated pastry into a rectangular
   shape about 1/4-inch thick.
6. Spread the honey on top, then sprinkle with raisins, almonds, pecans, and walnuts.
7. Beginning at the long end, carefully roll up the pastry; shape the log into a
   wreath to fit into a 6-cup round baking dish sprayed with nonstick spray.
8. Set the dish in the slow cooker, and cook on HIGH for 3 or 4 hours, or until
   golden brown.

Tip: This recipe is lovely as a late-morning snack. Prepare the pastry the
night before, refrigerate, and roll out and cook as soon as you get up.

Madame M.'s Chocolate Upside-Down Cake

QuickEase

*Kiss your diet goodbye, but say hello to a warm chocolate cake drenched
in sauce and ready to be polished off with ice cream.*

Serves 8

2 cups flour	1/4 teaspoon salt
1 1/2 cups sugar	1 cup milk
1/3 cup plus 2 tablespoons unsweetened cocoa powder	1/3 cup butter, melted
4 teaspoons baking powder	1 cup brown sugar
	1 cup boiling water

1. In a mixing bowl, combine the flour, sugar, 1/3 cup cocoa powder, baking powder, and salt.
2. Stir in the milk and butter, mix well, and transfer to slow cooker.
3. In a small bowl, combine the brown sugar and remaining 2 tablespoons of cocoa powder.
4. Sprinkle the mixture on top of the batter.
5. Pour the boiling water over the top.
6. Cook on **HIGH** for 2 hours, or until a toothpick inserted into the center of the cake comes out clean.

Tip: This is an excellent dessert on a hot summer day when you want cake, but don't want to turn on the oven.

So Much to Make . . .

There are 525,600 minutes in a year, and it seems, during every 1 of them, we're making something. We make money, mortgage payments, and ends meet. We make phone calls, appointments, and to-do lists. We make a point, a difference, a go of it. We make the grade, the final cut, the scene. We make a name for ourselves, and we make fools of ourselves. We make mountains out of mole-hills, and we make light of things. We make up our minds, good on our promises, and we make time, conversation, and friends. We make waves, we make do, we make-believe . . . and we make beds. Which leads me to my final thought. With all the things we have to make in this lifetime, why not make the best of it, and make eyes at your man, make a beeline for the bedroom, and make love and dinner at the same time? Darling, it makes sense.

Index